it is a secondary source

2. the elements of protien. are 22 animo acides ✗

0

3. Adults need 8 asenshall acids.
children need 10 asenshall animo acids.

animo acids are in good
ans one on more of the
acids are in short supply.

H.B.V. :-
cheese. ✓ Presentation
L.B.V. :- v.poor.
barley. ✓
peas, beans.

James Martin
Home Economics
Notes 5.1
Option 2
Book 1 Mrs Baxter

James Martin's GREAT BRITISH DINNERS

James Martin's
GREAT BRITISH DINNERS

Photography by Jean Cazals

MITCHELL BEAZLEY

Introdu

Loads of books
most pretty trad
raised on Sunda
Dick. And when
what you'll fin
traditionally Bri
overseas, like Cl

ALL DAY BREAKFASTS

Bacon Buttie

IF THERE WERE ONE MEAL I could request before I died, it would be my Gran's bacon buttie. She's no longer with us, but if I could make a buttie as well as she could, I would be a very rich man.

SERVES 2

30g (approx. 1oz) dripping
8 slices streaky smoked bacon
4 slices bloomer or pain
  de campagne
40g (1½oz) butter
2 ripe tomatoes, sliced
black pepper, to taste

Warm a large pan on the stove and add the dripping. Separate the bacon and add to the pan – watch out for the fat spitting out of the pan.

While the bacon is cooking, toast the bread, either on a griddle or under the grill. When the bacon is nice and crispy, remove from the pan. Add the butter to the pan and melt.

Dip the bread into the pan and then place on to the plates and build up the sandwich with the bacon and sliced fresh tomatoes. Pour over the rest of the juices from the pan, grind over some pepper, top with the other slice of bread and serve.

Sausage and Ketchup Sarnie

SAUSAGES ARE A TRADITION IN BRITISH COOKING, as is tomato ketchup, and although Heinz ketchup tastes great, the home-made stuff tastes even better. Give it a go: you may be surprised.

SERVES 2

1 tsp ground allspice
250ml (9fl oz) cider vinegar
8 tbsp demerara sugar
1.5kg (3lb 5oz) ripe tomatoes, diced
1 bay leaf
1 tsp English mustard
1 clove garlic, chopped
1 tbsp tomato purée
a dash of Worcestershire sauce
a dash of Tabasco sauce (optional)
450g (1lb) sausages
4 slices bread

To make the ketchup, put all the ingredients except for the sausages and bread into a large pan and bring to the boil, stirring all the time. Reduce the heat and simmer for about 40 minutes, stirring occasionally to make sure it doesn't stick to the bottom of the pan. Blitz in a liquidiser and pass through a fine sieve. Pour into a sterilised bottle and keep in the fridge.

To serve, grill or fry the sausages until cooked. Spread the ketchup on 2 slices of bread, then top each of these slices with sausages and another slice of bread.

My Dad's Cheese on Toast

MY FATHER TAUGHT ME THIS RECIPE – it's proper cheese on toast. This has to be one of the first culinary skills people master when they leave home!

SERVES 4

4 slices brown bread, toasted
25g (1oz) butter, softened
225g (8oz) Cheddar cheese, grated
3 tbsp double cream
a dash of Worcestershire sauce
a dash of Tabasco sauce (optional)
salt and pepper, to taste

Pre-heat the grill to its highest setting.

Spread the toasts with the butter.

Put the cheese in a bowl and add the cream, Worcestershire sauce, Tabasco (if using) and seasoning. Mix well. Spoon the mixture on to the buttered toasts.

Place the toasts under the grill, and then grill until the cheese starts to bubble on the top and turn golden brown. Remove and eat immediately.

Beef Burgers with Bacon

ALTHOUGH BEEF BURGERS ARE USUALLY THOUGHT TO BE AMERICAN, so many of us have grown up eating them, either from frozen, bought from one of the burger chains or – best of all – home-made, that they have attained British status.

SERVES 4

675g (1½lb) minced beef
1 tsp French mustard
salt and pepper, to taste
1 shallot, finely diced
1 clove garlic, finely diced
1 tbsp chopped flat-leaf parsley
1 egg

To cook and serve:

1 tbsp olive oil
25g (1oz) butter
4 rashers bacon
a handful of lettuce leaves, shredded
4 burger buns

Combine all the burger ingredients in a bowl. Form into 4 oval-shaped patties.

Sauté the patties in a hot pan in the olive oil and butter for 3-4 minutes on each side. While sautéing, grill the bacon until cooked through.

Place the salad leaves in your bun and put the burger and then bacon on top of the leaves.

Rib-eye Steak with Herbs and Mustard served with Honeyed Oven Chips

NOTHING BEATS SIRLOIN STEAK, deep-fried onion rings, peas and jacket potatoes or chips. This is just a more up-to-date version of our classic steak and chips. It uses rib-eye steak that is now, thankfully, found in most stores and butchers.

SERVES 4

4 rib-eye steaks
olive oil
salt and pepper, to taste
8 tbsp Dijon mustard
120g (4½oz) chopped herbs (parsley,
* coriander, basil, thyme,*
* chervil, etc)*
1 lemon, quartered

Honeyed oven chips:
500g (1lb 2oz) Estima potatoes,
* peeled*
4 tbsp runny honey
1 tsp thyme, chopped
1 clove garlic, chopped
4 tbsp olive oil

Pre-heat the oven to 200°C/400°F/gas mark 6.

For the chips, cut the potatoes into large, chip-sized pieces. Mix together the honey, thyme and garlic in a bowl. Whisk in the olive oil and use the mixture to coat the potatoes well.

Season the chips and place on a baking tray in the oven for 35-45 minutes.

Meanwhile, heat a griddle pan until it is very hot. Brush the steaks with a little olive oil and season with salt and pepper. Seal on the griddle and cook to taste.

Once cooked, brush the steaks with mustard and dip into the herbs. Slice each steak into 4-6 slices, arrange on a plate and serve with chips and a lemon quarter.

Asparagus Spears with Poached Egg and Tarragon Butter

I PRESENTED A SHOW for UK Food on asparagus and was lucky enough to visit a farm in Sussex. The season for English asparagus normally runs from May to June, for about six weeks. The most amazing thing I found at the farm was that it seemed like you could see the asparagus stalks growing; the farmer told me it was common to finish picking the field one day and then to go back to start picking again almost immediately as the asparagus grows so quickly.

SERVES 4

20-25 asparagus spears, trimmed
salt
1 tbsp white wine vinegar
4 eggs
100g (3½oz) butter
juice of 2 lemons
2 tbsp chopped tarragon
4 slices brioche, toasted

Steam the asparagus over plenty of boiling water for 3-5 minutes, depending on the thickness of the spears.

Bring a pan of salted water to the boil and add the vinegar. Whisk to make a whirlpool. Once it's settled crack an egg in the middle. Simmer for 2-3 minutes, remove and keep warm. Repeat with other eggs.

Melt the butter in a pan and stir in the lemon juice and tarragon. Pile 5-6 spears of asparagus on to each toasted brioche. Top with a poached egg and spoon on the butter sauce.

Gammon with Pineapple Salsa

AN UP-TO-DATE GAMMON AND PINEAPPLE, but do you know where I think the best gammon and pineapple can be tasted in the UK? In truckers' roadside cafés. Gammon with a tinned grilled pineapple ring, HP Sauce and some chips may not be the lowest-cholesterol dish in the world, but it tastes fantastic!

SERVES 4

4 slices gammon
6 pineapple rings, fresh or tinned
  with natural juice, chopped
juice of 2 limes
1 red chilli, de-seeded and chopped
1 tbsp roughly chopped mint
2 tbsp olive oil

Grill or fry the slices of gammon until cooked.

Mix the remaining ingredients together for the salsa. Serve with chips, potato wedges or vegetables and a generous of serving of salsa on the side.

Plain and Sweet Omelettes

I'M LUCKY ENOUGH TO have a local farmer deliver fresh eggs to me each day. But when doing my research for this book, I learned a simple thing that we take for granted, such as the standard British egg, has not always been British at all. In 1900, we imported 2 billion fresh eggs from as far away as Eastern Europe, so they can't have been that fresh, can they?

SERVES 1-2

Plain omelette:

3 fresh, free-range eggs
salt and pepper, to taste
25g (1oz) unsalted butter

Sweet omelette:

3 fresh, free-range eggs
25g (1oz) unsalted butter
100g (3½oz) fresh raspberries
3 tbsp fresh raspberry coulis
icing sugar

Smoked haddock omelette:

3 fresh free-range eggs
salt and pepper, to taste
25g (1oz) unsalted butter
50g (1¾oz) cooked un-dyed smoked
  haddock, flaked

Have ready a 20cm (8-inch) omelette pan. Beat the eggs lightly with some salt and pepper (leave out the seasoning if you're making a sweet omelette).

Heat the pan, then add the butter. When it melts, swirl it around the pan to coat the bottom. Add the eggs and shake the pan to spread them out evenly. Use a fork to draw the edges of the egg towards the centre, allowing unset egg to run to the sides. Continue until the egg is neatly set but still soft, with a little liquid on top. Take off the heat.

If you're not making a plain omelette, now add either the raspberries or the haddock to one half of the omelette, then flip the opposite side over it. Turn the omelette out of the pan on to a plate. Serve the sweet omelette with the sauce and a sprinkling of icing sugar.

Crumpets

I THINK THIS IS a real Yorkshire thing, although they have them in Lancashire as well. I call them crumpets, but in some areas they are called muffins. This recipe shouldn't be confused with the Scottish crumpet, which uses a thin pancake batter and is very different.

SERVES 4

500g (1lb 2oz) plain flour
15g (½oz) table salt
15g (½oz) fresh yeast
650ml (1 pint 3fl oz) warm water
butter for cooking

Sieve the flour and salt together into a bowl.

In a separate bowl, mix the yeast with 5-6 tbsp of the warm water.

Whisk the rest of the water with the flour and salt and then stir in the yeast mixture.

Cover and allow to rest in a warm place to rise. After 15-20 minutes, the batter is ready. If it is a bit too thick, loosen with a little warm water.

Warm a non-stick pan on the stove and lightly butter some metal crumpet rings or scone cutters. Melt some butter in the pan, too.

Place the rings in the pan and pour a little of the batter into each one, half filling them with the batter.

Cook on a gentle heat until holes appear in the top and the mixture starts to dry slightly around the edge. Turn over, remove the ring and cook lightly on the other side.

Chive Blinis with Smoked Salmon and Crème Fraîche

THIS IS THE FIRST DISH I remember making at catering college, and a must for any canapé tray. It's sometimes poshed up with a spoonful of caviar, but it's at its best when freshly made, and served with sliced smoked salmon and some thick, creamy crème fraîche.

SERVES 4

Blini:

5 egg whites
175g (6oz) plain flour
200ml (7fl oz) milk
1 egg, beaten
1 egg yolk
1 tsp bicarbonate of soda
salt and pepper, to taste

To cook and serve:

butter, for cooking
200g (7oz) smoked salmon
100g (3½oz) thick crème fraîche
2 tbsp finely chopped chives

Whisk the egg whites until stiff.

Mix together the remaining blini ingredients, then carefully fold the egg whites into the mixture.

Using a teaspoon, spoon the mixture on to a very hot, lightly buttered, heavy-bottomed frying pan and cook in a little butter for approximately 2-3 minutes on each side, until golden brown. When bubbling, flip over with a palette knife.

Cut the smoked salmon into small strips. Arrange a squiggly shape of salmon on each blini and add a teaspoon of crème fraiche and a sprinkling of finely chopped chives.

Oatcakes

I SUPPOSE THE MAIN REASON WHY OATS are thought to be Scottish is that they are the country's most successful cereal crop. There's a saying that Scottish housewives are born with a rolling pin under their arms; it's not to whack men with, but because of their love for baking. You can use finer flour for a lighter biscuit, but I like the old recipes.

MAKES 16 BISCUITS

100g (3½oz) medium fine oatmeal
pinch of salt
25g (1oz) butter, melted
3 tbsp water
plain flour, for dusting

Pre-heat the oven to 180°C/350°F/gas mark 4. Place the oatmeal and salt in a bowl and stir in the melted butter. Mix in enough water to create a firm, pliable dough.

Sprinkle the worktop with flour and knead the dough for a few minutes. Roll out the dough until it is about 3mm (⅛ inch) thick and cut out large round cakes. On each one, mark out 6 to 8 segments on the surface, but not right the way through. Bake in the oven for 8-10 minutes, until golden brown. Serve with any cheese you like – as long as it's British.

Kedgeree

MY FATHER USED TO COOK THE BEST KEDGEREE, always for breakfast. The prawns are optional, but the curry powder is a must to kick-start the flavour. A little chopped green chilli will give it the same kick if you don't have any curry powder.

SERVES 4

750ml (1 pint 6fl oz) milk
500g (1lb 2oz) undyed smoked
  haddock
40g (1½oz) butter
1 onion, finely chopped
175g (6oz) long grain rice
1 tsp medium curry powder
1 handful frozen cooked prawns,
  defrosted
salt and pepper, to taste
3 soft-boiled eggs, shelled, quartered
2 tbsp chopped flat-leaf parsley

Put the milk in a pan and bring to the boil. Add the haddock, making sure it is covered by milk, and simmer for 2 minutes. Take off the heat and allow to cool slightly. Flake the fish and pick off any bones and skin. Reserve the milk.

In a heavy-bottomed pan, melt 25g (1oz) of the butter and fry the onion for 2-3 minutes. Add the rice and curry powder, then the milk. Stir well. Bring to a gentle simmer and cook for 20-25 minutes, until the rice is cooked. Add a little more milk if it begins to dry out.

When the rice is cooked, add the haddock, then the prawns. Be careful when stirring not to break up the haddock too much. Season and put in a serving dish. Arrange the soft-boiled eggs around the edge, sprinkle with the parsley and top with a good knob of butter.

Pancakes with Honeycomb

I REMEMBER HATING BEES from the moment, when I was a kid, that my father decided it was a good idea to visit a local honey farm in the north Yorkshire moors. The heather-flavoured honey was great, but what of those mad people who, daily, had to face what seemed like certain death to collect it? Since then, I have tried to avoid going anywhere near bees again – that is, until I did a series called *Delicious* for UK Food, and had to go and get the honey myself! Dressed in my so-called sting-proof bee suit, I walked towards the wooden box. As I lifted out the tray of honey, the entire bee population descended on me. They stung me everywhere – and I mean everywhere! After running from them for what seemed like miles and swearing like I've never done before, *then* the bee-keeper warned me that bees don't like to be disturbed in the evening and when it's overcast and about to rain… Anyway, this recipe is a tribute to all you bee-keepers. Oh, and by the way, I think you're all bloody mad!

SERVES 2-3

Pancakes:

1 large egg

a pinch of salt

100g (3½oz) plain flour

300ml (10fl oz) cold milk

2 tbsp melted butter, plus extra for cooking

Honeycomb butter:

100g (3½oz) unsalted butter, softened

85g (3oz) honeycomb

2 tbsp runny honey

Make the pancakes by mixing together the egg, salt and flour and then slowly whisking in the milk. Just before cooking, mix in the melted butter.

Heat a heavy-bottomed saucepan on the stove. Add a small knob of butter and place a spoonful of the batter in the centre of the pan. Swirl the pan to coat the base with the pancake.

Place the pan back on the heat to cook the base of the pancake. Once the base is cooked, either flip the pancake over or use a palette knife to turn it, then cook the other side. Continue until all the batter is used up. Keep the pancakes warm.

To make the honeycomb butter, place all the ingredients in a food processor and blend until smooth. This will keep in a covered container in the fridge.

Serve 2-3 pancakes per portion topped with a spoonful or so of the fragrant butter.

Orange Marmalade

THOUGHT TO BE ENGLISH, orange marmalade was first made in Dundee in Scotland in about 1770. The Keiller Company there is one of the oldest producers of this fantastic product, but if you fancy giving it a go, here's an old recipe my gran and auntie once used. You must, however, use bitter, or Seville, oranges to give it that real 'just-like-Granny-used-to-make' taste.

MAKES ABOUT 1.4KG

550g (1lb 4oz) Seville oranges
juice of 1 lemon
1.4 litres (2½ pints) water
1.1kg (2lb 7oz) granulated sugar

To sterilise the jam jars, place them in a large pan and cover then with cold water. Bring to the boil and simmer for 10-15 minutes. Remove from the water and leave upside down to dry.

Halve the oranges and, with a spoon, scoop out the insides, leaving the pith behind.

Place the orange juice, membrane and pips in a food processor and blend. Once the mixture is smooth, pass through a sieve into a large pan.

Using a tablespoon, scoop out as much of the pith from the peel as possible and then cut the peel into very thin strips. Add to the juice, then add the lemon juice and water. Bring to the boil and simmer for about 1-1½ hours, until the peel is tender and the mixture has reduced by half.

Add the sugar and mix over a low heat until it has dissolved. Boil for about 10 minutes, removing any froth on the surface with a large spoon.

After 10 minutes, spoon a little of the marmalade on to a cold plate – it should be like jelly. If it is still runny, cook for a further 5-10 minutes.

Leave to cool slightly before filling, sealing and labelling the sterilised jars.

Chunky Strawberry Jam

I FIND MAKING JAM is one of the most rewarding things you can do, as you get to use the fruit at its best when it is in season and you reap the rewards throughout the rest of the year. That is, if you make enough – I never seem to as I keep deciding it makes a nice gift for someone!

MAKES 1.2KG

600g (1lb 5oz) jam sugar
juice and finely grated zest
  of 1 lemon
1kg (2lb 4oz) fresh strawberries,
  hulled and cut in half if large

To sterilise the jam jars, place them in a large pan and cover them with cold water. Bring to the boil and simmer for 10-15 minutes. Remove from the water and leave upside down to dry.

Place the sugar and the juice and zest of the lemon in a large pan and heat slowly until the sugar has melted.

Add the strawberries and stir gently. Bring to the boil and cook for 3-4 minutes, or 10 minutes if you prefer a thicker style of jam.

Leave to cool slightly, skimming off any froth with a clean spoon. Spoon into sterile jam jars, seal and label.

Hot Cross Buns with Blueberries

HOT CROSS BUNS ARE TRADITIONALLY baked for Good Friday and are thought to originate from pagan times. The spices used are allspice, cinnamon and cloves, or a mixture of them. Having been a pastry chef for about 8 years, I should be giving you a recipe for hot cross buns but, be honest, would you make them? Would you hell! So here is a great way to use them as a nice breakfast or dessert (not forgetting, of course, the 'true' way to eat them – toasted with butter – but I don't need to tell you that!).

SERVES 2

250ml (9fl oz) milk
15g (½oz) caster sugar
2 eggs
knob of butter
2 hot cross buns (or brioche)

For the blueberry sauce:
300g (10½oz) blueberries (or
* strawberries)*
45g (a good 1½oz) caster sugar
a splash of port or orange juice

To serve:
honeyed cream, crème fraîche,
* clotted cream or ice cream*

Put the milk and sugar into a bowl and, using a whisk, beat in the eggs. Leave to one side.

Prepare the fruit sauce by mixing together all the ingredients, crushing the fruit lightly to allow the juices to run.

Heat the butter in a pan. Slice the hot cross buns in half, dip into the eggy mixture, and cook in the butter for about 2 minutes on each side.

Remove the buns from the pan and place on a serving plate. Pile the blueberry sauce on top of the bottom half of each bun, top with 2 spoonfuls of cream or ice-cream, then add the lid of the bun. Serve immediately.

SOUPS, TARTS & TERRINES

Watercress Soup

WATERCRESS IS NEAR TO MY HEART. I am lucky enough to live in a part of England where watercress is famous. Hampshire, in particular Alresford, is the home of the famous 'watercress line' that used to deliver freshly cut watercress from the beds up to London. Sadly, this doesn't happen any more – instead, the cress travels by road. But the line does still exist and, for a small fee, you can travel a stretch of it in the original steam train and carriage. Watercress is grown in beds fed by spring water from underground. It needs a constant flow of this water to grow, and is available most of the year. Don't just use a sprig of it on the plate as a garnish; it's food in its own right and should be used as such. It's brilliant in sandwiches, makes great soups and is delicious in a fab pesto-style sauce due to its peppery taste.

SERVES 4-6

1 onion, sliced
2 cloves garlic, chopped
25g (1oz) butter
1.2 litres (2 pints) chicken stock
450g (1lb) Estima potatoes, peeled and diced
2 bunches watercress
freshly grated nutmeg, optional
200ml (7fl oz) double cream
salt and pepper, to taste

In a heavy-bottomed saucepan, fry the onion and garlic in the butter until softened but not coloured.

Add the stock and potatoes and bring to the boil. Simmer for 15-20 minutes, until the potatoes are cooked.

Chop up the watercress (leaves and stalks) and add to the soup with the freshly grated nutmeg, if using.

Simmer for 2-3 minutes before blending in a food processor in batches, adding the cream as you go.

Return to the pan to heat through gently and season with salt and pepper.

Leek, Potato and Stilton Soup

A CLASSIC SOUP with that most classic of all British ingredients: Stilton, the king of cheeses. Stilton has conquered the world, but is still exclusively made in seven dairies in Leicestershire, Nottinghamshire and Derbyshire. The best Stilton is made in the summer, with summer milk, which gives it a creamy yellow colour. It is usually sold at Christmas time. When buying Stilton, look for evenly distributed veins and a good contrast between the blue veins and the creamy cheese.

SERVES 4

1 chicken stock cube
600ml (1 pint) hot water
100ml (3½fl oz) white wine
1 medium leek, split, washed and
   thinly sliced
1 shallot, finely chopped
2 cloves garlic, finely chopped
1 large baking potato, peeled and
   finely chopped
125g (4½oz) strong Stilton
125ml (4fl oz) double cream
salt and pepper, to taste
1 tbsp parsley, chopped
1 packet of shop-bought croûtons

Place the stock cube, water and wine in a pan and bring to the boil. Add the leek to the pan with the shallot, garlic and potato. Cover and cook for 10 minutes.

Add the Stilton and cook for 4-5 minutes to melt the cheese. Add the cream, salt and pepper and blend.

Warm the croûtons. Serve the soup hot, sprinkled with the parsley, and offer the warmed croûtons separately.

Quiche Lorraine

THIS IS ONE OF THE FIRST DISHES that I cooked as a young chef at Castle Howard, when I was about eight or nine. It reminds me of the garden fêtes and village shows where wars were waged between grannies, aunties and the W.I.: rolling pins at dawn over the best sponge cake and scone in the show. But it didn't end there; there were also the best vegetables and flowers. I can remember the men who tended their plants throughout the year moaning about the bronze they had just won and back-stabbing the gold-medal winner.

SERVES 4

Pastry:
175g (6oz) plain flour, plus extra for dusting
salt, to taste
75g (2¾oz) butter, plus extra for greasing
water

Filling:
250g (9oz) English cheddar, grated
4 tomatoes, sliced (optional)
200g (7oz) bacon, chopped
5 eggs, beaten
100ml (3½fl oz) milk
200ml (7fl oz) double cream
salt and pepper, to taste
2 sprigs of fresh thyme

Sift the flour together with a pinch of salt in a large bowl. Rub in the butter until you have a soft breadcrumb texture. Add enough water to make the crumb mixture come together to form a firm dough, and then rest it in the fridge for 30 minutes.

Roll out the pastry on a lightly floured surface and line a 22cm (8½ inch) well-buttered flan dish. Don't cut off the edges of the pastry yet. Chill again.

Pre-heat the oven to 190°C/375°F/gas mark 5.

Remove the pastry case from the fridge and line the base of the pastry with baking parchment and then fill it with baking beans. Place on a baking tray and bake blind for 20 minutes. Remove the beans and parchment and return to the oven for another 5 minutes to cook the base.

Reduce the temperature of the oven to 160°C/325°F/gas mark 3.

Sprinkle the cheese into the pastry base and add the sliced tomatoes if you are using them. Pan-fry the bacon pieces until crisp and sprinkle them over the top.

Combine the eggs with the milk and cream in a bowl and season well with salt and pepper. Pour over the bacon and cheese. Sprinkle the thyme over the top and trim the edges of the pastry. Bake for 30-40 minutes, or until set.

Remove from the oven and allow to set. Trim the pastry edges to get a perfect edge (top cheffy tip there), then serve in wedges.

Asparagus Tart

ASPARAGUS HAS A VERY SHORT SEASON in the UK: only about six to eight weeks in May and June. It's best eaten with melted butter, using your fingers, but is also great in a tart, cooked with a Quiche Lorraine filling.

SERVES 4

Pastry:

400g (14oz) shortcrust pastry, ready-made (or 1½ times the quantity on page 31)
a little flour, for dusting
10g (¼oz) butter

Filling:

4 eggs
1 egg yolk
1 shallot, finely chopped
400ml (14fl oz) crème fraîche
salt and pepper, to taste
2 tbsp chopped flat-leaf parsley
100g (3½oz) Gruyère cheese, grated
400g (14oz) asparagus, blanched and cold

Roll out the pastry on a lightly floured surface and line a 25cm well-buttered flan ring. Leave the excess to hang over the edge. Chill for 30 minutes.

Pre-heat the oven to 190°C/375°F/gas mark 5.

Remove the pastry case from the fridge. Line the base of the pastry with baking parchment and fill with baking beans. Place on a baking tray and bake blind for 20 minutes.

Remove the beans and parchment from the pastry case and return to the oven for another 5 minutes to cook the base.

Reduce the temperature of the oven to 160°C/325°F/gas mark 3.

For the filling, beat the eggs, egg yolk and shallot together with the crème fraîche and season well. Fold in the parsley and half the cheese and spoon the mixture on to the base of the tart. Top with the asparagus and cover with the remaining cheese.

Trim the pastry around the edges. Bake for a further 30 minutes, until set, and serve warm.

Pork Terrine with Apricots and Pistachios

A GREAT DISH MADE EVEN SIMPLER by the use of good-quality pork sausages. Don't use cheap, poor-quality sausages for this or it will be a disaster. I'm using a terrine to cook it in, but you could use a bread loaf tin or even an ovenproof bowl. I've used Lincolnshire sausages, which I find are a good mix of fat and pork flavoured with sage and spices, but you could use any flavour you like. If you want a gamey flavour, use venison or game sausages, but remember: always go for quality, quality, quality in meat.

SERVES 4

Terrine:
olive oil
250g (9oz) streaky bacon
4-5 large sausages, Lincolnshire
  are best
10 sage leaves, chopped
1 tbsp flat-leaf parsley, chopped
100g (3½oz) dried apricots,
  chopped
75g (2¾oz) shelled pistachio nuts,
  chopped
salt and pepper, to taste

Salad:
2 oranges, peeled and segmented
50g (1¾oz) wild rocket
1 large potato, peeled, cooked
  and diced

Dressing:
8 tbsp plum sauce (you can make
  your own or the Chinese stuff
  from the supermarket is OK)
3 tbsp olive oil
salt and pepper, to taste

Prepare the terrine mould by brushing it with olive oil and lining it with streaky bacon, leaving 5-6cm (¼-½ inch) overlapping the edge of the mould.

Pre-heat the oven to 180°C/350°F/gas mark 4.

Make the filling by removing all the meat from the sausage skins (discard the skins). Add the sage leaves, flat-leaf parsley, apricots and pistachio nuts and mix well with plenty of salt and pepper. Pile the meat mixture into the terrine mould and press down well.

Fold the bacon over the meat and cover with either a lid or aluminium foil. Place in a bain-marie half-filled with hot water and cook in the pre-heated oven for 60 minutes.

Press down with a weight, cool, then place in the fridge to go cold.

For the salad, mix the orange segments with the rocket leaves and diced potato. For the dressing, mix the plum sauce with the olive oil and season well with salt and pepper.

Remove the terrine from the container and cut into slices. Serve on the centre of a plate with the salad around it and the dressing spooned over the top.

Baked Cheese in a Box

PUBS ARE A GREAT SHOWCASE FOR BRITISH FOOD, and that's where I got the idea for this. The Red Lion Pub in Stourbridge, Kent, serves fantastic food and great British beers. I had this baked cheese there with a loaf of bread to dunk into it, and it was well worth the 200-mile round trip!

SERVES 4

1 Bonchester or English Camembert
in a box
salt and pepper
extra virgin olive oil
½ tsp chopped fresh thyme,

To serve:
fresh crusty bread

Pre-heat the oven to 190°C/375°F/gas mark 5.

Remove the cheese from the box and, if the box is held together only with glue, staple it together as the glue will melt in the oven.

Take a sharp knife and cut the top off the cheese – just the skin. Then place the cheese back in the box, cut side up.

Season, drizzle with olive oil and sprinkle with fresh thyme. Put in the oven for 10-15 minutes until cooked through and brown on top.

Remove from the oven and serve with warm, crusty bread. It's a bit like a dip really; sort of a fondue thing.

ROASTS, PIES & BAKES

Roast Leg of Lamb

MINT SAUCE IS, of course, the true classic accompaniment to roast lamb. However, I once tried this combination while working at Antony Worrall Thompson's restaurant in the late 1980s. I was hooked. He made it with lamb shanks that were cooked overnight, and the combination is to die for.

SERVES 4

1 leg of lamb
6 cloves garlic, cut into slivers
3 large sprigs of rosemary
a small tin of anchovies
olive oil

Pre-heat the oven to 180°C/350°F/gas mark 4.

Make small cuts all over the meat and insert a sliver of garlic, a small piece of rosemary and half an anchovy fillet into each cut until all the ingredients are used up.

Drizzle with a little olive oil and roast in the oven, allowing 20 minutes per 450g (1lb) for meat that is pink in the centre, 25 minutes if you prefer it more well done.

Once the joint is cooked to your liking, remove and allow to rest before you carve the meat.

Roast Sirloin of Beef

ROAST BEEF WITH YORKSHIRE PUDDING is the best meal in the world, full stop. But then I *am* Yorkshire born and Yorkshire bred: strong in the arm and bloody good at making Yorkshire puddings!

SERVES 4

1 x 2.25-2.7kg (5-6lb/3 ribs)
  sirloin of beef on the bone
1 onion, quartered
1 tbsp plain flour
salt and pepper, to taste

To serve:
Yorkshire pudding (see page 56)

Pre-heat the oven to 240°C/475°F/gas mark 9.

Place the beef upright in a roasting tin, tucking in the onion quarters by the side.

Dust the flour liberally over the surface of the beef. Finally, season with some salt and pepper. This floury surface will help to make the fat very crusty, while the onion will caramelise to give the gravy a rich colour and flavour.

Place the joint in the oven. After 20 minutes, turn the temperature down to 190°C/375°F/gas mark 5, and continue to cook for 30 minutes for rare beef, plus 45 minutes for medium-rare or 60 minutes for well done.

While the meat is cooking, baste with the juices at least three times. To see if the beef is cooked to your liking, insert a thin skewer and press out some of the juices; the red, pink or clear colour will indicate to what stage the beef is cooked.

Remove the cooked beef to a board for carving and leave it to rest for at least 30 minutes before serving. During this resting time you can make the Yorkshire puddings. Pour any juices that are released from the beef into the gravy.

Roast Loin of Pork with Five Vegetables

A MUST FOR A SUNDAY LUNCH: roast loin of pork with crackling, roast potatoes, a quartet of other vegetables, and gravy.

SERVES 4

*1 x 1.8-2kg (4-4½lb) loin of
  pork with the skin on*
2 tbsp white wine vinegar
1 tbsp sea salt
1 tbsp chopped thyme
vegetable oil, lard or dripping
*900g (2lb) King Edward potatoes,
  peeled and cut into chunks*
salt and pepper, to taste
300g (10½oz) cauliflower florets
200g (7oz) carrots, chopped
200g (7oz) green beans, trimmed
300g (10½oz) broccoli florets
2 tbsp Marmite
150ml (5fl oz) red wine
600ml (1 pint) chicken stock
50g (1¾oz) butter

Pre-heat the oven to 180°C/350°F/gas mark 4.

Taking a sharp knife, score the skin of the pork 12-15 times. Rub the vinegar over the skin, then mix together the salt and thyme and rub into the skin.

Place in a roasting tray with some fat and roast in the oven for about 2 hours, basting every 15 minutes or so.

After about an hour, pour some of the fat juices into another tray and heat until smoking hot. Add more fat if necessary.

Season the potatoes with salt and add them to the hot fat, spooning it over to make sure each piece is covered. Cook in the oven until crisp and brown, which will take about 40 minutes, turning occasionally.

While the meat is in the oven, pre-cook the vegetables separately in plenty of boiling salted water. Begin with the cauliflower, then remove and plunge into cold water. Do the same with the carrots, beans and broccoli – in this order. Once they are all cooked and cooled, set aside until needed.

Once the meat is cooked, remove from the tray and leave to rest. Pour off the excess fat.

To make the gravy, place the oven tray on the stove and add the Marmite, red wine and stock. Boil to reduce by about half, stirring. Add half the butter and some seasoning before passing through a sieve. Keep warm until needed.

To serve, remove the roast potatoes and transfer to a serving dish. Reheat the vegetables in boiling salted water, tip into a serving dish and dot with the remaining butter. Remove the crackling, break into pieces and carve the meat. Pour the gravy into a jug.

Pot-roasted Shoulder of Pork with Chilli and Beer

GOOD PORK IS SO HARD TO FIND nowadays. Supermarkets seem to sell pork that has been bred to run the 100 metres rather than for flavour. Why have our tastes changed? We seem to want pork with no fat on it. I visit the man I consider to be the best pork producer in the country, Martin Martindale, who is based in Hampshire and sells his pork at local farmers' markets. Get there early though, before me! No Linford Christie pigs here, this is the best-tasting pork I've ever had.

SERVES 8

1 x 2.7-3.25kg (6-7lb) small, whole boned shoulder of pork, with the skin on
10 cloves garlic, crushed
salt and pepper, to taste
juice of 3 lemons
4 tbsp dried red chillies
3 tbsp olive oil
300ml bottle of bitter

Salsa verde:
10g (¼oz) capers
10g (¼oz) gherkins
4 spring onions
30g (about 1oz) mixed fresh herbs (chervil, basil, mint and parsley)
juice of 1½ lemons
2 tbsp extra virgin olive oil
salt and pepper, to taste

Pre-heat the oven to 230°C/450°F/gas mark 8.

Using a small sharp knife, score the whole skin of the shoulder of pork with deep cuts about 5mm (¼ inch) wide.

Mix the garlic with the salt, pepper, lemon juice, chillies and oil. Rub and push this mixture into and over the skin and on all the surfaces of the meat.

Place the shoulder on a rack in a roasting tin and pour the bottle of bitter into the base. Roast for 45 minutes, or until the skin begins to crackle and turn brown. Baste the shoulder once or twice while cooking, turn the oven down to 180°C/350°F/gas mark 4 and leave the meat to pot-roast for 3-4 hours.

The shoulder is ready when it is completely soft under the crisp skin. You can tell by pushing with your finger: the meat will give way and might even fall off the bone.

To make the salsa verde, chop the capers, gherkins, spring onions and herbs finely, then mix with the lemon juice and oil. Season well.

Serve each person with some of the crisp skin, meat cut from different parts of the shoulder and a spoonful of the salsa verde. I think this is best served cold with hot new potatoes.

Sugar and Clove-glazed Gammon

I REMEMBER WHEN I WAS A KID my gran used to buy me a couple of slices of York ham from Scott's Butchers in York (which has some fantastic pork and great pork pies, by the way). They'd always give her a free ham bone for the dog: a six inch high Yorkshire Terrier. It's a wonder the bloody thing wasn't the size of a horse! Mind you, it did live to a ripe old age. I was always told that, originally, York hams took their flavour from smoke from the oak sawdust that was around when they were building York Minster. This recipe doesn't go to that extreme, but it's a must for any buffet at Christmas.

SERVES 20-25

1 x 5-6kg (11-13lb) whole gammon
3 tbsp English mustard
30 cloves
4 tbsp demerara sugar
6 tbsp runny honey

Pre-heat the oven to 160°C/325°F/gas mark 3.

Soak the gammon in a sinkful of cold water overnight. (Ask your supplier how long you should soak it, as gammon pieces vary).

Remove from the water and pat dry. Put into a large oven tray and cover with foil.

Put in the oven for about 3½-4½ hours, or about 20 minutes per 450g (1lb), depending on the size of your joint.

Half an hour before the end of the cooking time, remove from the oven and turn the temperature up to 220°C/425°F/gas mark 7.

Remove the foil and peel off the skin, being careful not to burn yourself (rubber gloves can help here).

Using a sharp knife, score the fat in a criss-cross pattern all over the gammon. Rub the gammon with mustard and stud with the cloves, then sprinkle with the demerara sugar.

Drizzle with honey and return to the oven for about 20-30 minutes, until golden brown and well glazed. Keep basting with the juices in the pan and allow to cool before serving.

Roast Chicken with Tapenade

YEAH, YEAH, BEFORE WE START: corn-fed and organic chickens do have a better flavour than the normal fare, but my Gran didn't use them, nor did my mum or my auntie, so they have no place in this book. (Come to think of it, we had chickens that my Dad used to breed in our yard at home...) Stuffing the chicken under the skin creates flavour and helps keep the meat nice and moist. My girlfriend regularly stocks her fridge with what she calls an emergency chicken, just in case anyone pops round for something to eat. However, she has only cooked for me once in a year, so maybe this recipe will tempt her into using one of those emergency birds, though I doubt it...

SERVES 4

1 x 2kg (4lb 8oz) chicken
175g tapenade, bought-in or made
  as below
1 lemon, halved
1 bulb garlic, halved
salt and pepper
extra virgin olive oil

Tapenade:
200g (7oz) black olives, stoned
1 clove garlic
1 onion
3 tbsp capers
6 anchovy fillets
a small bunch of flat-leaf parsley
juice of 1 lemon
extra virgin olive oil
salt and pepper, to taste

Pre-heat the oven to 190°C/375°F/gas mark 5.

To make the tapenade, finely chop the olives, garlic, onion, capers, anchovy fillets and parsley. Mix in the lemon juice and enough oil to make a paste-like texture. Season well with salt and pepper.

Starting at the neck end of the chicken, push your fingertips between the skin and flesh to form a pocket. Spoon the tapenade between the flesh and skin, and pat down so that it spreads evenly.

Place in a roasting tin, squeeze over the lemon juice and then place the lemon halves around the chicken. Place the garlic into the body cavity. Season and drizzle with oil.

Roast in the oven for about 70-80 minutes, until the chicken is cooked through, basting the skin every 10 minutes with its own juices.

Serve slices of chicken with a spoonful of tapenade on the side.

Spiced Pot-roasted Chicken

JUST A LITTLE TWIST to make the standard roast chicken taste a little different.

SERVES 4

1 x 2kg (4½lb) roasting chicken
60g (2¼oz) butter
8 tbsp dark soy sauce
6 tbsp runny honey
2 cinnamon sticks
4 cloves garlic, halved
2 star anise
175ml (6fl oz) dry sherry
350ml (12fl oz) chicken stock

Pre-heat the oven to 200°C/400°F/gas mark 6.

Wipe the chicken. Melt the butter in a casserole dish, add the chicken and brown the bird on all sides. Sit breast-up in the casserole and pour over the soy sauce and honey. Add the cinnamon, garlic and star anise to the base of the pan and pour in the sherry and stock.

Place the casserole on the stove and bring to a simmer. Then cover the dish loosely with foil and put into the pre-heated oven. Cook for about 80 minutes, uncovering and basting with the juices every now and then, until the chicken is cooked through.

When cooked, remove the chicken and leave to rest in a warm place. Strain the juices into a clean pan and boil to reduce.

Serve the chicken, cut into pieces rather than carved, with the reduced juices, rice and a salad.

Roast Turkey with Cream Cheese and Coriander

MY GOD, A CHEF'S NIGHTMARE: how to make turkey taste nice and cook it without drying it out. Firstly, start by buying the right bird. I find Norfolk Blacks are the best, but generally you won't find them in a supermarket. You can get them from good butchers, but remember to order early for Christmas. They're reared on a small scale and are free range. Their black feathers give them a distinctive dark pitting of feather stumps on the skin when plucked, which is probably why supermarkets don't sell them as it doesn't look the same as pretty white skin. Inserting the cream cheese like this will help keep the meat nice and moist during cooking.

SERVES 8-10

1 x 4.5kg (10lb) oven-ready turkey
1 bunch of parsley, stalks removed
250g (9oz) cream cheese
*1 bunch of coriander, stalks
  removed*
4 tbsp olive oil
salt and pepper, to taste

Pre-heat the oven to 180°C/350°F/gas mark 4.

Place the turkey on a board and carefully lift the skin up at the neck. Work your hand under it to ease it completely away from the breast.

Process the parsley in a blender until chopped. Add the cream cheese and gradually add the coriander, blending between each addition until smooth. Finally, add 1 tbsp of olive oil and blend well. Alternatively, chop the herbs as finely as you can and mix with the cream cheese and olive oil.

Press the cream mixture into the space between the breast and skin of the turkey. Pull the skin back into place over the cheese mixture, press to re-shape and smooth over.

Place the turkey in a roasting tin and drizzle with the rest of the olive oil. Season well with salt and pepper.

Roast for 20 minutes per 450g (1lb), or until the juices run clean when the thickest part of the leg is pierced with a knife. Baste the turkey with the pan juices after 45 minutes.

Cover with foil and leave to stand for 15 minutes before carving.

Pork Pie

THIS PIE TASTES FANTASTIC, and while it is cooking, your kitchen will be filled with the most mouth-watering aromas. It is my belief that, no matter where you are, you can judge how good a butcher is by his pork pie. I first acquired my taste for them after buying one from Scotts Butchers in York, a family-run company. Although the main spice in a pork pie is usually pepper, other spices such as mace, cinnamon, nutmeg, coriander and ginger can also be added; the selection varies from recipe to recipe, so you can pick and choose. My dad would have made me eat this pie with Branston pickle but, after 16 years of having to eat it like that, I just like it with a bag of crisps. You can make this as one large pie or two smaller ones.

MAKES 1 15-20CM PIE

Pastry:
250g (9oz) lard
300ml (½ pint) water
900g (2lb) plain flour, plus extra
* for dusting*
a good pinch of salt
butter, for greasing

Filling:
900g (2lb) lean pork mince or
* diced pork shoulder*
2 medium onions, diced
2 pinches of nutmeg
salt and pepper, to taste
100ml (3½fl oz) dry white wine
1 egg, lightly beaten
1 x 284ml tub ready-prepared
* chicken stock*

Make the pastry by bringing the lard and water to the boil in a pan. Sieve the flour into a food processor and add the salt. While the processor is on, pour the hot water and lard on to the flour and blend until you have a smooth dough. When finished, turn the dough out into a large bowl and allow to cool slightly.

Grease a 15-20cm pie mould with butter. On a lightly floured surface, roll out two-thirds of the pastry and line the pie tin, leaving an overhang. Don't worry if it's a bit like working with clay; it will be worth it in the end. Place in the fridge to set. Keep the remaining pastry covered and warm.

Pre-heat the oven to 180°C/350°F/gas mark 4. To make the filling, mix the pork with the onions and season with nutmeg, salt and pepper. Add the wine and mix. Pile the filling into the pastry crust.

On a lightly floured surface, roll out the remaining pastry, using a little extra flour if it's sticky. Put it on top of the pie, then trim and crimp the edges with your thumbs. Brush the top with some of the beaten egg.

Bake in the oven for 40 minutes. Carefully remove from the tin and brush the edges with the lightly beaten egg again. Return to the oven for a further 20-30 minutes to set the sides and cook through.

Remove from the oven and allow to cool. Warm the chicken stock, then make a little hole in the top of the pie. Pour as much stock as the pie will take in through the hole. Chill to set.

Chicken and Leek Pie

A TASTY PIE, making good use of the under-rated leek. Serve with a green vegetable such as broccoli.

SERVES 4

225g (8oz) ready-made shortcrust
  or puff pastry
1 egg, beaten

Filling:
4 chicken breasts (without skin or
  wing bone)
olive oil
250g (9oz) shallots
2 leeks, washed
25g (1oz) unsalted butter
300ml (½ pint) crème fraîche
150ml (5fl oz) chicken stock
salt and pepper, to taste

Pre-heat the oven to 200°C/400°F/gas mark 6.

Seal the chicken breasts in a hot pan in a little oil or char-grill on both sides. Set aside to rest.

Pan-fry the shallots in a little oil, then bake in the pre-heated oven for 10 minutes. Chop the leeks and pan-fry in the butter until soft.

Heat the crème fraîche and stock together and season with salt and pepper. Cut the chicken into fork-sized pieces and add to the stock mixture. Simmer for 5 minutes, then add the leeks and shallots. Put into a suitably sized pie dish.

Roll out the pastry and cut a strip to go around the rim of the pie dish. Top the pie with the piece of pastry and crimp the edges to seal. Decorate if you like, and brush with the beaten egg.

Bake in the oven for 30 minutes.

Shepherd's Pie

WHY IS IT THAT PEOPLE get confused about which meat goes in cottage pie and which goes in shepherd's pie? I will never know. Do you see many shepherds with a herd of cows in a field?

SERVES 4

1 onion, cut into chunks
50g (1¾oz) swede, cut into chunks
100g (3½oz) carrots, cut into chunks
½ tsp ground cinnamon
1 tsp chopped fresh thyme
1 tbsp chopped flat-leaf parsley
10g (¼oz) plain flour
350g (12oz) minced lamb
salt and pepper, to taste
1 tbsp tomato purée
425ml (15fl oz) vegetable stock

Topping:
900g (2lb) Desirée or King
  Edward potatoes
75ml (2½fl oz) double cream
50ml (2fl oz) semi-skimmed milk
40g (1½oz) Cheddar cheese, grated
25g (1oz) Parmesan, freshly grated

Pre-heat the oven to 140°C/275°F/gas mark 1.

Place the onion, swede and carrots into the bowl of a food processor. Add the cinnamon, herbs and flour and whiz everything until it is finely chopped, but not puréed. Place in a casserole dish, add the lamb and season well.

Heat the tomato purée and stock together to boiling point. Stir this into the casserole and mix together well. Place the casserole over a gentle heat and bring it up to simmering point. Cover with the lid and place it in the oven for 2 hours.

About 30 minutes before the end of the cooking time, peel the potatoes, cut them into chunks and put them into a pan of cold water. Bring to the boil and then simmer for 20 minutes, or until tender.

Drain the potatoes thoroughly, then mash them well. Add the cream, milk and some salt and pepper. Continue to beat the potatoes until they are light and fluffy.

Take the casserole out of the oven and turn up the temperature up to 200°C/400°F/gas mark 6.

Transfer the meat to a shallow dish and cover it evenly with the mashed potato. Cover the potatoes with grated Cheddar and sprinkle with the Parmesan.

Return the pie to the oven for a further 15 minutes, or until the top is golden and crusty.

Steak and Kidney Pie

GREAT PUB FOOD is one of the joys of where I live, and steak and kidney pie is one of my faves. There are so many variations of this classic. Some say it should have oysters, beer or stout in the mix, but I think this one is the nicest I've cooked. Besides, would you want me to give you a recipe with beef, kidneys and oysters topped with pastry? I don't think so. Although purists say this pie should be made with shortcrust pastry on the top, I feel puff pastry makes a much better topping.

SERVES 4

300g pack of puff pastry
1 egg and 1 extra egg yolk,
  beaten together

Filling:
25g (1oz) beef dripping or 2 tbsp
  vegetable oil
700g (1lb 9oz) stewing beef, diced
200g (7oz) lamb kidney, diced
2 medium onions, diced
8 button mushrooms, halved
25g (1oz) plain flour
½ tbsp tomato purée
700ml (1¼ pint) beef stock
150ml (5fl oz) red wine
salt and pepper, to taste
2 tbsp chopped fresh parsley
a dash of Worcestershire sauce

Heat the dripping or vegetable oil in a large frying pan, and use to seal the beef in batches until well coloured. Browning the meat is really important, as it gives the pie a really deep golden colour.

Brown the kidney in the same pan, then add the onions and mushrooms and cook for 3-4 minutes.

Return all the meat to the pan, then sprinkle the flour over to coat the meat and vegetables. Add the tomato purée, stock and red wine to the pan, stir well and bring to the boil. Turn the heat down and simmer for 1½ hours without a lid on. If the liquid is evaporating too much, add a little more stock.

Shortly before the end of the cooking time, pre-heat the oven to 220°C/425°F/gas mark 7.

Add some salt and pepper, the parsley and Worcestershire sauce to the filling. Leave to cool slightly.

Place the cooked meat mixture into a pie dish. Roll out the pastry to 5mm (¼ inch) thick, and 5cm (2 inches) larger than the dish you are using. Cut a strip of pastry to fit around the edge of the pie dish, and stick it down using a little water. Brush the top with beaten egg.

Use the rolling pin, lift the pastry and place it over the top of the pie dish. Trim and crimp the edges with your fingers and thumb. Brush all over the surface with the beaten egg and decorate with any pastry trimmings. Brush any decorations with beaten egg. Bake for 30-40 minutes. I love this with either mash, peas or carrots or – to hell with it – have all three!

Sausagemeat, Red Pepper and Apricot Stuffing Balls

THESE MAKE A GOOD accompaniment for a roast chicken or turkey, full of interesting flavours. I quite like to eat them by themselves too.

SERVES 4

450g (1lb) sausagemeat
2 tbsp ground almonds
2 roasted red peppers (canned or in a jar), finely chopped
8 dried apricots, finely chopped
salt and pepper, to taste
1 tsp dried mixed herbs
olive oil for greasing

Pre-heat the oven to 180°C/350°F/gas mark 4.

Place the sausagemeat in a bowl. Add the ground almonds, red peppers and apricots. Season with salt and pepper and add the dried mixed herbs. Mix well.

Roll into 16 balls and place on a greased baking sheet. Brush with olive oil and bake for 30 minutes.

Corned Beef Hash

Corned beef and Spam were the basis of so much food we ate as kids, but they're not deemed trendy any more. Or are they? I cook corned beef hash to remind me of what my auntie used to cook for me. Served with a little salad, it is a satisfying snack that can be eaten at any time of the day. It's good for breakfast, perhaps topped with a fried egg. It can also be made into little patties – when the mix might need to be bound with an egg. In America, corned beef hash is served with ketchup (see page 10) or chilli sauce.

SERVES 4

2 onions, chopped
1 tbsp fresh thyme leaves
25g (1oz) butter
1 tsp Marmite
350ml (12fl oz) beef stock
150ml (5fl oz) red wine
375g (13oz) corned beef
2 tbsp chopped flat-leaf parsley
salt and pepper, to taste

Filling:
250g (9oz) potatoes, peeled
milk, for mashing potatoes
25g (1oz) butter
50g (1¾oz) Cheddar cheese, grated
25g (1oz) breadcrumbs

Pre-heat the oven to 200°C/400°F/gas mark 6.

Boil the potatoes in plenty of simmering, salted water. When they are just cooked, remove from the heat and cool in cold water. Drain, dice and leave to one side.

In a large frying pan, fry the onions and thyme in the butter for about 3 minutes. Add the Marmite, stock and red wine and reduce by half. Add the corned beef, parsley and and some salt and pepper and cook for 5-10 minutes, breaking it up with a fork.

Season the cooled potatoes and mash them thoroughly with some milk and butter.

Place the corned beef mixture into an ovenproof dish and top with the mashed potatoes. Grate the cheese and mix together with the breadcrumbs. Sprinkle the mixture over the mashed potatoes and bake for 20 minutes to cook through and brown the top.

Serve with a dressed green salad.

Toad in the Hole

WELL, IF I CAN'T MAKE YORKSHIRE PUDDINGS I shouldn't be writing this book. I'm going to give you some top tips. Make the batter well in advance, so it can rest, and make sure the dish is hot before you add the batter to it. When in the oven, keep the door closed for at least 20 minutes. So there you go: good luck and happy rising of your Yorkshires! You can make large toads or individual ones.

SERVES 6

6 sausages, such as Cumberland
  or Lancashire
olive oil
3 tbsp grain mustard
25g (1oz) beef dripping or vegetable
  oil

Yorkshire pudding:
225g (8oz) plain flour
8 medium eggs
salt and pepper, to taste
600ml (1 pint) milk
1 tbsp chopped fresh thyme leaves

First, make the Yorkshire pudding batter by placing the flour and all the eggs into a bowl with some salt and pepper. Whisk until smooth and stir in all the milk and the chopped thyme.

Cover and place in the fridge for at least 2 hours, or preferably overnight.

Pre-heat the oven to 220°C/425°F/gas mark 7, and place a large Yorkshire pudding tin in the oven to warm.

Sauté the sausages in a hot pan with a little oil to colour them. Remove them from the pan and coat in the mustard. Remove the hot tray from the oven, add the dripping and heat again.

Add the sausages on the centre of the tray and, while the tray is hot, pour in the batter.

Bake for 25-30 minutes, until risen and golden brown.

STEWS, POTS & SPICY FOODS

Traditional Lancashire Hot Pot

THIS MUTTON OR LAMB STEW made with sliced potatoes should, I think, be on every British pub menu.

SERVES 4

900g (2lb) best end and middle
neck of British lamb, chopped into
large bite-sized pieces
1 tbsp vegetable oil
butter
4 lamb's kidneys, cored, skinned
and chopped quite small
350g (12oz) onions, cut into
1cm pieces
1 tbsp plain flour
600ml (1 pint) hot lamb stock
½ tsp Worcestershire sauce
salt and pepper, to taste
1 bay leaf
2 sprigs of thyme
900g (2lb) potatoes, peeled and cut
into 2cm (¾ inch) slices

Pre-heat the oven to 170°C/325°F/gas mark 3.

Trim the lamb of any excess fat. Heat the oil with a little butter in a large frying pan until it is very hot, then brown the pieces of lamb two or three at a time. As they cook, put them into a casserole (3.5 litre/6 pint capacity). Brown the pieces of kidney too, and tuck these in among the meat.

Fry the onions, adding a little more butter to the pan if necessary, for about 10 minutes, until they turn brown at the edges. Stir in the flour to soak up the juices and gradually add the hot stock and Worcestershire sauce, stirring or whisking until the flour and liquid are smoothly blended. Season with salt and pepper and bring it up to simmering point. Pour it over the meat in the casserole.

Add the bay leaf and thyme, then arrange the potato slices on top in an overlapping pattern. Season the potatoes and add a few dots of butter to the surface.

Cover with a tight-fitting lid and cook in the oven for 1½ hours. You can remove the lid and brush the potatoes with a little more butter, then place under the grill to crisp up if you like. Otherwise, turn the heat up during the last 15 minutes of cooking time in the oven and remove the lid. Remove the bay leaf and sprigs of thyme before serving.

Beef Stew and Dumplings

HOW MANY PEOPLE HAVE TASTED this dish and thought the dumplings ended up like rubber bullets? Not if you follow this recipe! The secret to a good stew, I think, is sealing the meat well before adding the stock. This, if done properly, will give the stew increased flavour and a much better dark colour.

SERVES 4

4 tbsp olive oil
450g (1lb) stewing beef, diced
75g (2¾oz) chicken livers, cut
  into chunks
100g (3½oz) celery, diced
100g (3½oz) carrot, diced
½ leek, chopped
1 small red onion, diced
2 cloves garlic, crushed
150ml (5fl oz) good red wine
500ml (18fl oz) fresh beef stock
4 tinned anchovies, diced
salt and pepper, to taste
10 baby onions
15g (½oz) butter
8 sun-dried tomatoes, diced
10 new potatoes, cooked
4 tbsp fresh pesto
3 tbsp chopped flat-leaf parsley
4 tbsp torn basil

Dumplings:
125g (4½oz) plain flour
1 tsp baking powder
a pinch of salt
60g (2¼oz) shredded suet
1 tbsp chopped flat-leaf parsley
water

Pre-heat the oven to 140°C /275°F/gas mark 1.

Put 2 large pans on a high heat with a third of the olive oil in each and, when hot, brown the beef and livers in 1 pan and the vegetables and garlic in the other. Fry both until they are nice and brown.

Place the contents of both pans into a casserole dish and deglaze the pans with the red wine and beef stock. Add the liquid to the stewing dish.

Add the anchovies, season with salt and pepper and cook, with the lid on, in the oven for about 3 hours.

Meanwhile, make the dumplings. Sieve the flour, baking powder and salt together into a bowl. Mix in the suet and chopped parsley and enough water to form a slightly thick dough. Placing a little flour on your hands, roll the dough into small balls, remembering that they will swell as they cook in the stew.

At the end of the stew's cooking time, fry the baby onions in the remaining oil and the butter, season with salt and pepper and add to the stew with the sun-dried tomatoes and potatoes. Simmer for 5 minutes, then season well and add the pesto and herbs.

Remove the meat and vegetables from the liquid with the slotted spoon and keep warm in a dish, covered with foil, in the low oven.

Put the casserole over a high heat and, when bubbling, add the dumplings. Turn the heat down and poach gently for 20 minutes, as the dumplings will break up too much if they are allowed to boil.

Serve the stew with the dumplings.

Beef Stroganoff

THINLY SLICED BEEF IN a rich onion, mushroom and cream sauce, though Russian in origin, has become a classic, not just here in the UK but throughout Europe. Here, though, I've used minced beef; it's easier and less expensive – although it's a good idea to use good quality mince for this recipe. Like the goulash on page 64, this dish reminds me of my mother's food: food she placed in a big dish in the middle of the table with an even bigger bowl of pilaf rice.

SERVES 4

75g (2¾oz) butter
1 tbsp olive oil
2 small onions, sliced
1 clove garlic, crushed
175g (6oz) brown mushrooms,
  sliced
225g (8oz) best minced beef
1 tbsp paprika
1 tbsp French mustard
75ml (2½fl oz) double cream
salt and pepper, to taste
2 tbsp chopped flat-leaf parsley

To serve:
225g (8oz) fresh noodles, freshly
  cooked
a little butter
75ml (2½fl oz) sour cream

Heat a large frying pan on the stove and add the butter and olive oil. Fry the onions and garlic for about 5 minutes, until softened.

Add the sliced mushrooms, mince and paprika. Fry on a high heat to seal the mince. After 5 minutes, add the mustard and pour in the double cream. Bring to a gentle simmer before adding some salt and pepper.

At this point, remove from the heat and add the chopped parsley.

Butter the freshly cooked noodles, pile them on to plates, then spoon on the stroganoff and serve with a dollop of soured cream on the top.

Goulash

GOULASH IS, OF COURSE, Hungarian in origin, and was originally a beef soup. So why is this in a book on British food? Because, like dishes such as stroganoff and satay, it's a real classic that we have been brought up with. For me, it's the food mum cooked when I was a kid to get me used to spices and different flavours, the main spice here being paprika. Like all spices in those jars at home, paprika has a shelf life and a use-before date on the jar. The use-before date is not, as many of us might think, when the label has changed colour in the sun. Don't imagine that the dried thyme you bought 6 years ago and used once will still be OK to put into the pot!

SERVES 4

olive oil
700g (1lb 9oz) stewing steak, diced
30g (a good 1oz) plain flour
1 large onion, thinly sliced
2 cloves garlic, finely chopped
1 green pepper, deseeded and
  thinly sliced
1 red pepper, deseeded and
  thinly sliced
2 tbsp tomato purée
2 tbsp paprika
2 large tomatoes, diced
75ml (2½fl oz) dry white wine
1½ x 284ml tub of fresh beef stock
2 tbsp flat-leaf parsley, chopped
salt and pepper, to taste
150ml (5fl oz) sour cream

Pre-heat the oven to 160°C/300°F/gas mark 3

Heat a heavy-based saucepan with a little olive oil. Sprinkle the steak with the flour and brown well, in batches, in the hot pan. Set the sealed meat aside.

Sauté the onion, garlic and peppers in the same pan in a little more oil. Return the beef to the pan with the tomato purée and paprika. Cook for about 2 minutes.

Add the tomatoes, white wine and stock. Cook with a lid on in the oven for 1½ hours. Alternatively, cook it on the hob on a gentle heat for about an hour, removing the lid after 45 minutes.

Before serving, add the chopped parsley and season well with salt and pepper. Stir in the soured cream.

P.S: Thanks for the recipe, Mother!

Moussaka

WHY DO WE LIKE moussaka so much? Well, I think it's due to its origins – it's common to Turkey and Greece, which is where I first tasted this dish and fell in love with it. The traditional version would be cooked in a dish or a mould lined with cooked aubergine skins, and served either in the dish or turned out of the mould. Either way it's fantastic: that hot, bubbling mass of mince, aubergine and cheese. Mmm, delicious.

SERVES 4-6

4 aubergines
olive oil
½ onion, chopped
2 cloves garlic, crushed
675g (1lb 8oz) minced lamb
3 plum tomatoes, diced
a good pinch of powdered cumin
a good pinch of powdered cinnamon
150ml (5fl oz) red wine
2 tbsp chopped mint
150ml (5fl oz) chicken stock
200ml (7fl oz) white sauce (see page 67)
2 eggs, beaten
a pinch of nutmeg
salt and pepper, to taste
50g (1¾oz) mozzarella, grated
50g (1¾oz) Cheddar, grated

Pre-heat the oven to 190°C/375°F/gas mark 5.

Slice the aubergines, then fry them on both sides in a large pan with a little olive oil. Drain on kitchen paper.

To save on washing up, use the same pan with a little more olive oil to fry the onion and garlic. After 5 minutes, turn the heat up and add the lamb to brown it. Add the tomatoes.

Add the powdered cumin and cinnamon with the wine and sauté together to break up the tomatoes. Add the chopped mint and the stock in stages.

In an ovenproof dish, place the aubergines and minced lamb mixture in alternated layers, finishing with a layer of aubergines.

Combine the white sauce with the eggs, nutmeg and some salt and pepper. Spoon over the top of the aubergines, then scatter with the grated cheeses.

Bake for 25-30 minutes to colour the cheese and cook through.

Macaroni Cheese

THE SIMPLEST BAKED PASTA DISH OF ALL. You can bake it in one large dish or divide the mixture between smaller dishes. You could add sliced tomatoes to the mixture or put them on the top, and you can ring the changes by experimenting with different types of cheese.

SERVES 4

350g (12oz) macaroni
salt and pepper, to taste
100g (3½oz) Red Leicester, grated
2 tbsp fresh breadcrumbs
a little butter

White sauce:
25g (1oz) butter
25g (1oz) plain flour
300ml (½ pint) double cream or milk
a little nutmeg, freshly grated

Pre-heat the oven to 180°C/350°F/gas mark 4.

Cook the macaroni in a large pan of boiling salted water for about 15 minutes. Drain well.

Meanwhile, to make the white sauce, melt the butter and then stir in the flour. Add the cream or milk gradually, stirring all the time, until you have a thick sauce. Season with salt, pepper and freshly grated nutmeg.

Add most of the cheese to the sauce, saving some for the top.

Put the cooked macaroni into a 1 litre (1¾ pint) serving dish. Pour over the sauce. Top with the remaining cheese and the breadcrumbs. Dot with butter and bake for 20 minutes, until golden brown.

Serve with crusty bread.

Spaghetti Bolognese

BOLOGNESE, OR RAGU, is, of course, Italian – but it is also one of the UK's most often cooked dishes. So naturally it has its place in this book – and rightly so, as it's a fantastic sauce. To my mind, it gets even better after a few days in the fridge before being reheated for a midnight snack.

SERVES 6

25g (1oz) butter
8 rashers streaky bacon, diced
1 large onion, diced
1 large carrot, diced
3 garlic cloves, finely chopped
500g (1lb 2oz) minced beef
600ml (1 pint) red wine
½ tbsp tomato purée
1 x 284ml tub of fresh beef stock
400g (12oz) tinned tomatoes, or 6
  fresh tomatoes, chopped
1 tbsp flat-leaf parsley, chopped
a dash of Worcestershire sauce
salt and pepper, to taste

To serve:
325g (11½oz) spaghetti, freshly
  cooked
25g (1oz) butter
Parmesan, freshly grated

Heat a really large saucepan on the stove and add the butter.

Fry the bacon, onion, carrot and garlic for a few minutes, stirring all the time. Add the beef and cook for about 4 minutes to colour well, before adding the wine and tomato purée. Simmer for about 5 minutes.

Add the stock and tinned tomatoes (or fresh tomatoes if you are using them).

Simmer gently for 30-45 minutes before adding the parsley, Worcestershire sauce and plenty of salt and pepper.

Serve with freshly cooked, buttered pasta and some freshly grated Parmesan (not the ready-grated stuff in a cardboard tub!).

Chicken Kiev

A CLASSIC, THOUGHT TO HAVE ORIGINATED IN RUSSIA, although I doubt it somehow. However, wherever it comes from, this dish has got great flavour, and its a very celebratory type of meal.

SERVES 4

4 chicken supremes
3 eggs, beaten
200g (7oz) fine dry breadcrumbs
vegetable oil, for deep-frying
1 lemon, quartered lengthways

Garlic butter:
3 garlic cloves, finely chopped
3 tbsp finely chopped flat-leaf
  parsley,
1 tbsp finely chopped
  tarragon (optional)
125g (4½oz) butter, softened
salt and pepper, to taste
1 tbsp lemon juice

To make the garlic butter, put the garlic, parsley and tarragon (if using) in a blender with the butter. Season with salt, pepper and lemon juice. Blend to a smooth paste. Roll the butter in foil or cling-film and put it in the fridge.

Remove the skin from the first chicken supreme, laying it skinned side down. Detach the small fillet from the underside of the main fillet and cut this small fillet along its length and almost all the way through, folding it open before flattening it by beating it gently with a rolling pin. Put 15g (½oz) of the chilled garlic butter in the middle of the small fillet and wrap the meat around it. Repeat with the 3 other small fillets, returning all 4 to the fridge once you've finished.

Cut open each of the larger fillets in the same way, place them between plastic sheets and gently them beat out with a rolling pin. Lay a small buttered fillet in the middle of each larger fillet and wrap the escalope around it.

Dip in beaten egg and then in breadcrumbs. Repeat to give a double coating. At this point it is best to refrigerate them to allow the butter to harden again.

Heat to high a deep-fat fryer or a pan containing vegetable oil, and place the kievs in the hot oil, turning to allow 4-5 minutes cooking time on each side. It is important to cook and handle the kievs gently to stop them from falling apart.

When the chicken is cooked and a golden-brown colour, remove and drain very well on kitchen paper.

Serve each kiev with a wedge of lemon and some salad.

Coronation Chicken

A REAL CLASSIC THAT everyone must have tasted at some point, but there are loads of different recipes to choose from. I've found this one an easy and tasty way of making this dish.

SERVES 4-6

25g (1oz) butter
½ onion, finely chopped
3 tbsp curry paste
2 tbsp tomato purée
100ml (3½fl oz) red wine
juice of ½ lemon
4 tbsp apricot jam
300ml (10fl oz) mayonnaise
150ml (5fl oz) Greek yogurt
salt and pepper, to taste
6 chicken breasts, cooked,
  skins removed

In a small pan, heat the butter and then add the onion and cook for 3-4 minutes until softened. Add the curry paste, tomato purée, wine and lemon juice. Simmer, uncovered, for about 5 minutes, until the sauce is reduced. Strain and cool.

Add the apricot jam to the mixture with the mayonnaise, yogurt and salt and pepper to taste, and mix.

At this point you can leave the mixture like this, or do as I prefer to do: blend it until smooth. But I'll leave it up to you. Mind you, I never did mind creating more washing up!

Cut the chicken into fork-sized pieces. Spoon the sauce over the chicken and serve with bread or rice and a green salad.

Quick Chicken Tikka Masala

THEY SAY THIS IS BRITAIN'S favourite dish – which is exactly why it is here!

SERVES 4

1 x 2.5cm (1 inch) piece of root
 ginger, finely chopped
1 tsp ground turmeric
2 cloves garlic, finely chopped
1 red chilli, deseeded and
 finely chopped
1 tbsp finely chopped coriander
 leaves
juice of 2 limes
2 tbsp vegetable oil
salt and pepper, to taste
4 chicken breasts, skinned and
 sliced into strips
1 onion, finely chopped
300ml (10fl oz) double cream
juice of ½ lemon

In a large bowl, mix the ginger, turmeric, garlic, chilli, half the coriander, the lime juice, 1 tbsp of the oil, salt and pepper. Add the chicken slices and then stir well to make sure all the pieces are coated. Put in the fridge for 10-15 minutes.

Sweat the onion in a large pan with the remaining oil. Then add the chicken slices and all the marinade ingredients. Cook on a medium to high heat for 4-5 minutes.

Add the double cream and simmer gently for 3-4 minutes, until the meat is cooked through. Season and add lemon juice to taste, together with the remaining chopped coriander.

Serve with naan bread and/or boiled rice and a chilled beer.

FISH & SEAFOOD

Salmon Fish Cakes with Pickled Cucumber and Ginger Relish

FISH CAKES ARE WRONGLY thought to be made from poor-quality cuts of fish. But actually they should always be made using the best cuts. I've used salmon as it's readily available to us all, but fish such as haddock, smoked haddock, tuna, crab (see page 93) and cod are all brilliant for fish cakes.

SERVES 4

500g (1lb 2oz) King Edward
  potatoes, peeled and cut into
  large chunks
25g (1oz) butter
75ml (2½fl oz) single cream
1 tsp mild or medium curry
  powder
2 tbsp chopped parsley
1 large green chilli, deseeded and
  finely chopped
1 shallot, finely chopped
salt and pepper, to taste
500g (1lb 2oz) cooked salmon,
  bones and skin removed
4-5 tbsp plain flour, seasoned
2 medium eggs
150g (5½oz) dried breadcrumbs
corn or sunflower oil for deep-frying

Relish:
1 cucumber
25g (1oz) fresh root ginger
2 cloves garlic
juice of 2 lemons
3 tbsp groundnut oil
1 tbsp sesame oil
salt and pepper, to taste

Boil the potatoes in a saucepan filled with lightly salted water for about 15 minutes, or until tender. Drain well, then return to the pan. Mash with a fork or potato masher until smooth, beating in the butter, cream, curry powder, parsley, chilli, shallot and lots of salt and pepper. Leave to cool completely.

Meanwhile, check the salmon for any remaining bones, then flake. Mix the fish with the potato and shape into 8 round patties.

To coat the salmon cakes in breadcrumbs requires a methodical approach. Complete each of the 3 stages for all the cakes before moving on to the next stage. That way, you won't get too messy.

So, first coat each cake in seasoned flour, shake well and place on a plate. Beat the eggs in a wide shallow bowl, then dip each cake into the egg to coat evenly. Place the breadcrumbs in another wide bowl and coat each cake in the crumbs, pressing the crumbs on to coat the surface evenly. Shake off any excess and place on a plate. Chill in the fridge for about 30 minutes to 'set' the crumbs.

Meanwhile, make the relish. Peel the cucumber, cut it in half lengthways and scoop out all the seeds. Slice very thinly lengthways into ribbons. Put in a bowl. Peel and grate the ginger and garlic and add to the cucumber. Mix together the lemon juice and oils and pour over the cucumber. Season with salt and pepper. Leave to marinate while you cook the first cakes.

Heat the corn or sunflower oil to a depth of 1cm (½ inch) in a wide, shallow frying pan until you feel a good heat rising. Slide in the cakes using a fish slice. Cook for about 3 minutes, until crisp and golden on the underside, then turn and cook the other side.

Remove and place on kitchen paper. Serve the cakes with the relish.

Seared Salmon with Sesame Watercress Salad

A MODERN TWIST to a recipe that uses two great British ingredients: salmon and watercress.

SERVES 2

2 x 200g (7oz) salmon fillets (no skin or bone), cut on a slant
olive oil
50g (1¾oz) watercress
2 tbsp toasted sesame seeds
salt and pepper, to taste

Watercress dressing:
50g (1¾oz) watercress, blanched
25ml (1fl oz) rice wine vinegar
125ml (4fl oz) grapeseed oil

Make the dressing first. Blend together all the ingredients in a food processor and leave to one side for the flavours to infuse.

Heat a cast-iron griddle or frying pan on the stove until very hot and brush the salmon on both sides with a little oil. Season and then fry on both sides for 3-4 minutes.

While the fish is cooking, place the watercress on the plate and then put the cooked salmon in the middle.

Sprinkle the toasted sesame seeds over the top, drizzle with the watercress dressing and serve immediately.

Wild Salmon with Samphire

WILD SALMON IS AT ITS BEST in the summer, when samphire – one of the best accompaniments for it – is available. There are two types of samphire: rock and marsh. Marsh is found on tidal marshes around Britain, though it is most common in Norfolk; rock grows on – yes, you guessed it – rocky cliffs and slopes around the coast. They used to use marsh samphire as a source of soda when making glass. No glass-making here, but picked early in the season samphire can be eaten raw, blanched or pan-fried. I pickle it in vinegar in mid-season, when it is at its cheapest.

SERVES 4

500g (1lb 2oz) samphire
90g (3¼oz) butter, softened
2 tbsp olive oil
4 x 175g (6oz) wild salmon fillets, bones and skin removed
pepper, to taste

To cook the samphire, remove any of the woody roots with a pair of scissors and wash very well. Blanch in lots of boiling water for 1 minute and then refresh in a bowl of ice-cold water to retain the colour.

Meanwhile, melt 25g (1oz) of the butter in the olive oil in a hot non-stick pan and then fry the salmon fillets over a high heat for 5-6 minutes. Do not shake the fillets.

Allow the fillets to crisp on the underside, before turning over using a palette knife. Add another 25g of the butter and remove from the heat. The residual heat in the pan will continue to cook the fish.

Drain the samphire really well before reheating in a pan with the remaining butter. Season with pepper only, as the samphire is quite salty.

Place some samphire on the plate, top with the salmon and spoon over the warm, buttery juices.

Smoked Haddock Risotto
with Sautéed Black Pudding

YES, I KNOW: RISOTTO ISN'T BRITISH, but this is a great way of bringing two of our favourite foods, haddock and black pudding, together. Smoked haddock, the best I think being Finnan haddock, was once smoked over peat for eight to nine hours. Don't subject this dish to that dyed, glow-in-the-dark junk that is sometimes for sale. As for black pudding, I was brought up on it. I'm not explaining how it's made as it's a bit graphic. All I'm going to say is cook it for breakfast, lunch or dinner – if it's a good-quality black pudding, nothing can beat it!

SERVES 4

1 litre (1¾ pints) fresh fish stock
1 shallot, finely chopped
1 garlic clove, finely chopped
25g (1oz) butter
250g (9oz) arborio rice
50ml (1¾fl oz) dry white wine
225g (8oz) undyed smoked
  haddock, cooked and flaked
olive oil
150g (5½oz) black pudding, sliced
85g (3oz) mascarpone
100g (3½oz) Parmesan, freshly
  grated
4 tbsp chopped flat-leaf parsley
salt and pepper, to taste

Heat the fish stock in a pan to warm it, but do not boil.

Meanwhile, sweat the shallot and garlic in a pan with half the butter over a low-medium heat, but don't colour. Turn the heat down to low, add the rice and seal it for about 30 seconds. Add the wine and cook for a futher few seconds.

Add the warmed stock, little by little, stirring all the time. Simmer for about 12 minutes, until the rice is cooked but still a little crunchy, continuing to add the stock a little at a time. It's important that the stock in the pan is all used up at the point the rice is cooked, so be careful not to add too much stock. After 10 minutes, add the flaked smoked haddock.

Heat a frying pan until very hot with a little oil and the remaining butter. Seal the black pudding slices in this for a few minutes on both sides.

Mix the mascarpone and grated Parmesan into the risotto with the chopped parsley, and season well.

To serve, put the risotto on to the centre of the plate, top with a few slices of the black pudding, and serve immediately.

Fish Pie with Cheese and Mustard Pastry

JUST A TWIST ON fish pie. The cheese and the mustard are slipped in between a layer of puff pastry. Use salmon, cod, haddock or monkfish – and a handful of prawns if you're like my gran.

SERVES 4

1 shallot, chopped
1 tbsp olive oil
100ml (3½fl oz) fish stock
200ml (7fl oz) double cream
salt and pepper, to taste
675g (1lb 8oz) fish (see
  introduction for types of fish),
  cut into chunks
125g (4½oz) mushrooms, sliced
3 tbsp chopped chives
300g (10½oz) ready-to-roll puff
  pastry
2 tbsp grain mustard
4 slices Emmental cheese
1 egg, beaten

Pre-heat the oven to 200°C/400°F/gas mark 6. Firstly, sauté the shallots in a pan in the olive oil. After a few minutes add the fish stock and cream and bring to the boil. Season with salt and pepper and leave to one side.

Place the fish, mushrooms and chives in an oven-proof dish. Season and cover with the sauce.

Roll out the pastry until it is twice the size of your dish. Spread half of the pastry with the mustard and cheese. Fold the other half over the top to sandwich the mustard and cheese in the middle. Top the pie dish with the pastry.

Crimp the edges of the pastry and then brush it with the beaten egg. Bake for 25-30 minutes.

Once cooked, remove from the oven and serve. A good accompaniment is French beans sprinkled with some freshly cracked black pepper.

Goujons of Sole with Lemon

AS FAMOUS AS Chicken in a Basket. Give me this, some tartare sauce (see page 105) and a wedge of lemon, and I'm a happy man.

SERVES 4

450g (1lb) sole or lemon sole fillets, skinned
125g (4½oz) fine fresh breadcrumbs
½ tsp cayenne pepper
sunflower oil for deep frying
50g (1¾oz) plain flour
3 medium eggs, beaten
salt and pepper, to taste
2 lemons, cut into wedges

Cut each sole or lemon sole fillet into strips, on the diagonal, about 1cm (½ inch) thick. Mix the breadcrumbs with the cayenne pepper and leave to one side. Heat the oil in the fryer to 190°C/375°F.

Coat the fish in the flour, then dip first in the beaten egg and then in the breadcrumbs. Do a few pieces at a time, making sure all the fish is coated in each of the three dips.

Place a few of the goujons in the fryer at a time and cook for about 1 minute, until crisp and golden brown. Repeat until all the goujons are cooked. Once cooked, remove on to some kitchen paper to soak up the excess oil.

Pile the goujons in a dish or on plates, season, and serve with the lemon wedges. They're great with a mixed, dressed green leaf salad.

Kipper Paste on Toast

MANX KIPPERS ARE THE MOST widely known, I suppose, but Whitby kippers are my favourite – not because I'm a Yorkshire man, but because I think they are the best (although hard to find if you're not local). They have a strong, smoky flavour.

SERVES 4

2 pairs Craster or Isle of Man undyed kippers
plenty of slightly salted butter
3 tbsp double cream
salt and pepper, to taste
a pinch of cayenne pepper
juice of 1 lemon
4 slices brown bread

Place the kippers in a large jug or tray and immerse in boiling water. Leave for a few minutes before draining the hot water off and removing the skin and bones from the fish.

Weigh the flesh and blend, while still warm, with an equal amount of butter. Add the cream, then season with salt, pepper, cayenne and lemon juice. Serve spread on brown toast. This mixture will keep in the fridge for up to a week in an airtight container.

Grandad's Poached Haddock with Mustard

I LIKE THIS DISH how my grandad used to have it: with spuds straight from the garden and lashings of butter! Funny, but it was the only dish my Grandad would cook not just for himself, but for anybody who came to visit. From the age of five I can remember eating this waiting for what was coming next – 2 hours of me being batsman with him bowling Freddie Truman-style against the wall of my gran's kitchen. Funny how food brings back memories.

SERVES 2

1 fillet of undyed smoked haddock (my grandad used Finnan)
1 bay leaf
a few black peppercorns
½ onion, roughly chopped
500ml (18fl oz) milk
50g (1¾oz) butter
1 tbsp plain flour
2 tbsp Dijon mustard
2 tbsp chopped flat-leaf parsley
salt and pepper, to taste

Cut the haddock in half and place in a shallow pan. Add the bay leaf, black peppercorns and onion and cover with the milk.

Bring the milk to the boil and gently simmer for about 4-5 minutes to cook the fish.

Carefully remove the fish from the milk, preserving the milk, and keep the fish warm.

Melt the butter in a pan and then add the flour and stir over the heat for 15-20 seconds to make the base of a roux. Slowly add the warm milk, a little at a time, stirring all the time until you end up with a nice smooth sauce. You may not need all the milk. Add the mustard and parsley to taste and check the seasoning.

Place the haddock on the plate and spoon over the sauce.

Cod with Mashed Potatoes

SADLY, COD IS BECOMING A RARITY because of over-fishing, but you can still find it at a price. Cook it carefully, please!

SERVES 2

2 x 150-200g (5½-7oz) cod fillets
1 tbsp olive oil
15g (½oz) butter

Mashed potatoes:
600g (1lb 5oz) Maris Piper
 potatoes, peeled and quartered
salt and pepper, to taste
75g (2¾oz) butter, softened
100ml (3½fl oz) double cream
a little nutmeg, freshly grated

Put the potatoes in a pan and cover with water. Add a good pinch of salt and bring to the boil. Cook for about 20-25 minutes.

Meanwhile, heat the oil in a pan and fry the cod, skin-side down, for about 5-7 minutes, until the flesh is about three-quarters cooked (it should feel springy). Turn over, add the butter, and turn off the heat – the fish will continue to cook in the residual heat of the pan.

Once the potatoes are cooked, drain and place back in the pan. Mash with a masher and add the butter and cream a little at a time; this will stop any lumps appearing.

Season with salt, pepper and nutmeg and serve with the cod.

Cod with Honey-glazed Onions

I LOVE COD, although I cook it less these days. It is wonderful with potatoes, but fantastic spiked with the onions.

SERVES 4

6 large onions
3 cloves garlic
75g (2¾oz) butter
2 tbsp runny honey
a dash of white wine vinegar
salt and pepper, to taste
1 sprig of thyme
2 bay leaves
1 sprig of rosemary
4 x 150-200g (5½-7oz) cod steaks

Pre-heat the oven to 180°C/340°F/gas mark 4.

Slice the onions and garlic, and fry them together in 25g (1oz) of the butter for about 10 minutes until well caramelised. Add the honey and vinegar and season with salt and pepper.

Place the onion mixture into an ovenproof dish and top with the herbs.

Place the cod on top of the onion and season well. Place the remaining butter in pieces on top of the cod.

Cook the dish in the oven for about 15-20 minutes, depending on the thickness of the cod.

Take the fish out of the oven and remove the herbs. Serve with the onions and a dressed salad.

Deep-fried Cod

ALL HAIL, HARRY RAMSDEN – or at least as it was when I was a kid. I used to love queuing outside waiting to be served with the crisp, battered fish and floppy, buttered bread on chequered tablecloths. Alas, that has all changed. I can now say without doubt that the best fish and chips on the planet are to be found at Trencher's fish and chip shop in Whitby. Eat in or out, or do as I do and have one of each. Walk down the pier and sit on the seat at the end and, in the wind and cold, with your nose dripping on to the fish, munch away. That's how to eat fish and chips.

SERVES 2

vegetable oil for deep-frying
plain flour
salt and pepper, to taste
2 x 200g (7oz) cod fillet, boned
  (haddock if you prefer)

Batter:
225g (8oz) self-raising flour, sieved
300ml (10fl oz) lager

Heat the vegetable oil in the deep-fat fryer to 180°C/350°F.

Lightly season some flour with some salt and pepper. Dip the cod fillets into the flour, shake off any excess and leave to one side.

To make the batter, place the sieved flour in a bowl and slowly whisk in the lager until very thick and slightly gluey in texture. Season with salt. Dip the cod fillets in, one at a time, to coat well with the batter. If the batter falls off, it is too thick.

Place the battered cod into the deep-fat fryer very slowly, literally a couple of centimetres at a time. If you drop the fish in, it will sink straight to the bottom and stick!

Allow the fish to cook for 4-5 minutes before turning over, and cook until golden brown. This should take 10-12 minutes in total.

Once the fish is cooked, drain on kitchen paper and season well. Serve with chips, mushy peas, Sarson's vinegar and a wedge of lemon, if you wish.

Garlic Prawns

THE 1970S AND 1980S saw a huge rise in the popularity of garlic – from garlic prawns and garlic bread to breadcrumb-coated garlic mushrooms (whatever happened to them?). Living in Hampshire, I'm lucky enough to be close to the Isle of Wight, where a lot of British garlic is grown, thanks to the high density of light reflecting off the sea around the island.

SERVES 4

*20 cooked tiger prawns with
  tails on*
4 tbsp olive oil
4 cloves garlic, crushed
2 tbsp dry white wine
salt and pepper, to taste
2 tbsp chopped flat-leaf parsley
1 lemon, cut into quarters
1 loaf of crusty bread, warmed

Firstly, prepare the prawns by cutting each one through the length of the back. Pull out the dark vein and discard it. It's a bit fiddly, I know, but you will thank me for this when you eat them – the gritty bit you get in your mouth if this is not removed is the remainder of the prawn's last supper.

Heat a large pan on the stove. Add the olive oil and, when it's hot, add the garlic. Sauté for a few seconds, then add the prawns and white wine. Sauté well for about 45 seconds to 1 minute. Season with salt and pepper and add the parsley.

Serve straight away with wedges of lemon and some chunks of crusty bread so you can dunk it in the juices while eating. Oops: don't forget a bowl of warm water on the table for your fingers, as it can get a bit messy.

Tiger Prawns Steamed in Beer

I FIRST TASTED THIS DISH a few years ago in the States, and I thought it was fantastic but lacked real flavour. I decided this was probably due to the type of beer used. So, of course, I decided to use Yorkshire bitter instead of lager, and now it's a great dish that, for me, has got even better.

SERVES 4-6

350ml bottle of beer (not lager)
450g-675g (1lb-1lb 8oz) raw
  prawns, shells on
salt and pepper, to taste
olive oil

To serve:
2 lemons, cut into wedges
100ml (3½fl oz) mayonnaise
4-6 sprigs flat-leaf parsley

Heat a wok on a high setting. Place a bamboo steamer base (or an ordinary steamer) in the bottom of the wok and add 200ml (7fl oz) of the beer.

Season the prawns in a bowl and drizzle with a little olive oil. Place in the steamer basket with a lid on. Reduce the heat to moderate.

Steam for 5-6 minutes, until the prawns are cooked. Tip out the prawns into a serving bowl and serve with wedges of lemon and a bowl of mayonnaise. Top with sprigs of flat-leaf parsley.

Potted Shrimps with Melba Toast

THE FIRST THING I LOOK FOR at farmers' markets are potted shrimps. I have to – I don't know why – it's just my fix. I suppose it dates from the days when my parents took us to Blackpool and I first tasted the shrimps from Morecambe Bay.

SERVES 4

125g (4½oz) Danish unsalted
  butter
a good pinch of cayenne pepper
a good pinch of ground nutmeg
600ml (1 pint) peeled cooked shrimps
salt and pepper, to taste

To serve:
4 slices thin sliced white bread
green leaf salad, dressed
1 lemon, cut into wedges

Put the butter in a pan to melt with the cayenne and nutmeg. Once it has melted, add the shrimps. Mix over the heat and season. Put the shrimps in little pots or ramekin dishes and press down. Top with butter left in the pan and chill in the fridge.

To make the Melba toast, pre-heat a grill until it's nice and hot. Grill the bread on both sides until golden brown. With a sharp knife, remove the crusts, then slice in half horizontally. Put back under the grill, cut side uppermost, to toast. The edges will curl up to give the traditional Melba toast effect.

Serve the shrimps with salad, a lemon wedge and 2 slices of toast.

Prawn Cocktail

WHAT A STARTER! You may ask what the hell it is doing in this book. Well, I'll tell you. Name one starter that has been on a menu in both three-star restaurants and cafés. It must be one of our all-time favourite starters (although smoked salmon comes close). I remember eating this as a kid at the Berni Inn in York: defrosted prawns, iceberg lettuce, a quarter of tomato, a slice of cucumber, a wedge of lemon and Marie Rose sauce. And, of course, a must with prawn cocktail is brown bread and butter. Who said the British can't produce good food? I do have to say that I have brought it up-to-date slightly, but the taste remains much the same.

SERVES 6

900g (2lb) raw large prawns with
* shells on*
olive oil for frying
1 lettuce, preferably cos
25g (1oz) rocket leaves
1 ripe avocado
cayenne pepper

Sauce:
100ml (3½fl oz) mayonnaise
1 tbsp Worcestershire sauce
a dash of Tabasco sauce
2 tbsp tomato ketchup (see page 10)
juice of 1 lime

To prepare the prawns, heat the oil in a large, solid frying pan and shallow-fry them for 4-5 minutes until they turn a vibrant pink. Leave them to one side to cool. Reserve 6 in their shells for garnish and peel the rest. Take a small, sharp knife and cut along the back of each peeled prawn to remove any black thread.

To make the cocktail sauce, mix the mayonnaise with the rest of the ingredients. Stir and taste to check the seasoning. Keep the sauce covered with cling film in the fridge until it is needed.

Shred the lettuce and rocket finely and divide among 6 plates or glasses. Peel and chop the avocado into small dice and scatter this among the lettuce. Top with prawns and then the sauce. Sprinkle a dusting of cayenne pepper on top and garnish with 1 unpeeled prawn per serving.

Oysters and Guinness

GUINNESS WAS INTRODUCED TO THE WORLD in 1759 by Arthur Guinness in Dublin. But now, like so many beers, it is brewed all over the world, from Jamaica and Ghana to Canada and Australia. But real lovers of Guinness, like me, will know that the best pint is always going to be in a Dublin pub – a pint poured with time and care. And the best accompaniment is an oyster.

SERVES 4

12 fresh oysters
1 lemon, quartered
a pinch of cayenne pepper

To serve:
brown bread and butter
4 pints of Guinness

Wash and open the oysters.

Loosen the base of the oysters with a knife and arrange on crushed ice. Decorate with the lemon wedges and season with cayenne.

Serve with the bread and butter on the side and a pint of Guinness.

Crab Cakes

A FABULOUS TASTE OF THE SEA. Serve these crab cakes piping hot with some pickled cucumber and ginger relish (see page 74) underneath.

SERVES 4

500g (1lb 2oz) King Edward potatoes, peeled and cut into large chunks
salt and pepper, to taste
25g (1oz) butter
2 tbsp double cream
1 tsp mild or medium curry powder
2 tbsp chopped fresh coriander
1 large green chilli, deseeded and finely chopped
1 tbsp grated red onion
500g (1lb 2oz) flaked crab meat, preferably white meat
2-3 tbsp plain flour, seasoned
2 medium eggs, beaten
100g (3½oz) dried breadcrumbs
corn or sunflower oil, for deep-frying

Boil the potatoes in a saucepan of lightly salted water for about 15 minutes, or until tender. Drain well, and then return to the pan. Mash with a fork or potato masher until smooth, beating in the butter, cream, curry powder, coriander, chilli, onion and lots of salt and pepper. Leave to cool completely.

Meanwhile, check the crab meat carefully for any flecks of shell and discard. Mix the crab meat with the potato mixture, and then shape into eight neat round patties. If the mixture sticks to your hands, simply dip them in cold water.

To coat the crab cakes in breadcrumbs requires a methodical approach. Complete each of the three stages for all the cakes before moving on to the next stage. That way, you won't get too messy.

So, first dip each cake in seasoned flour, shake well and place on a plate. Beat the eggs in a wide shallow bowl, then dip each cake into the egg to coat evenly. Place the breadcrumbs in another wide, shallow bowl and dip each cake in the crumbs in turn, pressing the crumbs on to the surface to coat the cake evenly. Shake off any excess crumbs and place the crab cakes on a plate. Chill in the fridge for about 30 minutes to 'set' the crumbs.

Heat the oil to a depth of 1cm (½ inch) in a wide, shallow frying pan until you feel a good heat rising. Carefully slide in the crab cakes using a fish slice. Cook for about 3 minutes, until crisp and golden brown on the underside, then carefully turn and cook the other side. Remove and place on kitchen paper. (If you have a medium-sized frying pan, you may find it best to fry the crab cakes in 2 batches).

If not serving the crab cakes immediately, place uncovered in a warm oven so that the coating stays crisp.

VEGETABLES & EXTRAS

Classic Roast Potatoes

ROAST TATTIES, as my grandad would say, and I have to confess that this is my mum's way of cooking them. By the way, make loads of these potatoes, as they're great cold with Anchor butter – none of that poncey unsalted butter that chefs tell you is best.

SERVES 6

10 medium King Edwards, Maris
Pipers or Desirée potatoes
Maldon sea salt
50g (1¾oz) lard or dripping (cooking
oil if you don't have either)

Pre-heat the oven to 200°C/400°F/gas mark 6. Peel the potatoes and cut each one in half (into 3 if the potatoes are large). Place in a saucepan and cover with cold water and a good pinch of salt. Bring to the boil and simmer for a maximum of 3-4 minutes. Pour into a colander and allow to drain well.

Heat the lard or dripping in a roasting tray on the stove and fry the potatoes until they start to brown. Turn them occasionally. Sprinkle generously with salt and then roast for about 30 minutes, before removing and turning them in the tray in order to prevent them from sticking. Roast for another 30 minutes and remove. Serve immediately.

Jacket Potatoes

SOMETIMES A LITTLE OF WHAT HURTS YOU does you good – and a good knob of butter melting into jacket potatoes tastes fantastic.

SERVES 4

4 large baking potatoes
olive oil
rock salt or Maldon sea salt
75g (2¾oz) butter

Pre-heat the oven to 180°C/350°F/gas mark 4. Wash and dry the potatoes and prick each one about 8 times all over with a fork. Rub with olive oil and sprinkle with rock or sea salt.

Bake the potatoes in the oven for 1½-2 hours, until cooked. They should be crisp on the outside and soft in the middle.

Cut a cross in the top, then, using your fingers, squeeze in the middle to push the top out. Spoon on a good knob of butter.

Brussels Sprouts

THE OLD DAYS of putting the Brussels on at the same time as the turkey have, thankfully, long gone, because sprouts cooked properly with lots of melted butter can be a real joy to eat.

SERVES 4

1kg (2lb 2oz) Brussels sprouts
salt and pepper, to taste
butter

Trim off the outer leaves of the Brussels sprouts.

Bring a large saucepan of salted water to the boil. Place the sprouts in the water and bring back to the boil as quickly as possible. Simmer for 3-4 minutes, until just cooked but still with a bit of crunch.

Drain into a colander and place in a bowl with a knob of butter and a good twist of freshly ground black pepper.

Mushy Peas

Fish and chips can't be without them. There are so many recipes for mushy peas, but the old ones are still the best. Mushy peas can only be made with time on your side. They take one to two hours to cook, not 20 minutes; hence you don't see any of the boys or me on *Ready, Steady, Cook* making them. Oh no: these take time, but remember all good things come to those who wait.

SERVES 6

225g (8oz) dried marrowfat peas
1 tsp bicarbonate of soda
35g (1¼oz) butter
salt and pepper, to taste

In a large bowl, soak the peas in three times their volume of water with the bicarbonate of soda for at least 4 hours or, if you have the time, overnight.

Drain the peas, rinse under the tap, place on the stove in a large saucepan and cover with water. Cover and bring to the boil and, once boiled, reduce the heat and simmer the peas for 1½-2 hours, stirring from time to time.

The peas should be soft and mushy in texture but not too dry. If they are too wet, continue cooking over the heat with the lid off to dry out a little. Beat in the butter, season and serve.

Garlic Mushrooms

THERE WAS A TIME when to eat anything with garlic in it was considered a bit 'daring'. Now we just enjoy it, and it goes fantastically with mushrooms. Try different types of mushrooms: buttons would be good, too, as would some of the exotic cultivated varieties, such as oyster mushrooms.

SERVES 4

*600g (1lb 5oz) chestnut or brown
  cap mushrooms*
25ml (1fl oz) extra virgin olive oil
*4 cloves garlic, finely diced or
  crushed*
30g (1oz) butter
juice of ½ lemon
salt and pepper, to taste
2 tbsp chopped flat-leaf parsley

Clean the mushrooms. Heat the oil in a large frying pan and add the mushrooms. Fry for about 2-3 minutes over a high heat, stirring all the time.

Add the garlic and butter and cook for a further 2-3 minutes.

Finish by quickly stirring in the lemon juice and salt and pepper to taste and the chopped parsley.

Serve in a bowl with some lovely warm, crusty bread.

Mustard Pickle

PICKLES AND CHUTNEYS are not everyone's cup of tea, but they have to be a must in a book on British food. Look at Branston pickle and piccalilli. These, together with jams and marmalades, are staples for so many of us, but very few of us have a go at making them. This is an old recipe that I first used while at college. It takes a while to make, but it's worth it. My dad loves it with pork pie. I like it with a ploughman's or with some cold sliced meat, such as ham. But whatever you decide to serve with it, give it a go. Come back the pickle, I say.

MAKES ABOUT 1KG

225g (8oz) table salt
500g (1lb 2oz) baby onions
250g (9oz) cherry tomatoes
500g (1lb 2oz) cauliflower florets
500g (1lb 2oz) cucumber, deseeded
  and cut into large dice
1 tbsp capers
1 tsp celery seeds
125g (4½oz) butter
25g (1oz) plain flour
500ml (18fl oz) malt vinegar
125g (4½oz) caster sugar
1 tbsp turmeric powder
2½ tsp mustard powder
black pepper, to taste

Dissolve the salt in a large pan or bowl in about 4 litres (7 pints) of water and add the onions, tomatoes and cauliflower. Cover with cling film and keep in the fridge or in a cool place for 24 hours.

Drain, then add the diced cucumber, capers and celery seeds and put in a pan. Cover with 2 litres (3½ pints) of water and bring to the boil. Boil for 10 minutes.

Drain again and put the vegetables into a bowl.

In a separate pan, melt the butter, then add the flour and stir well over the heat to make a roux. Slowly add the vinegar, stirring all the time, and cook for a few minutes.

Add the sugar, turmeric powder and mustard powder, and season with black pepper before pouring over the vegetables. Put the vegetables into sterilised jars and seal.

Leave for at least 5 days before eating, so that the vegetables can absorb all the flavour.

Béarnaise Sauce

BÉARNAISE IS FRENCH, not British, but we have taken it to our hearts. It's one of what they call the 'mother sauces', the basis for others such as 'Choron' and 'Maltaise'. It's closely related to Hollandaise, based on butter and egg yolks, and has as many uses. It's wonderful with any fish dish and with meat (especially steak) and vegetables. In the best kitchens it's made with clarified butter and by hand – but my version is much easier. The secret of this Béarnaise is to make sure that the butter is bubbling when it is added to the egg yolks for the sauce to thicken.

SERVES 4

2 tbsp tarragon vinegar
50ml (2fl oz) white wine or water
1 tsp crushed white peppercorns
200g (7oz) unsalted butter
4 egg yolks
2 tbsp chopped tarragon
salt and white pepper, to taste
a squeeze of lemon juice

In a pan, heat the vinegar and wine or water with the peppercorns and bring to the boil. Simmer rapidly until the liquid has reduced by half. Strain out the peppercorns, return the liquid to the pan and bring back to the boil.

In another pan, gently melt the butter. Add the reduced liquid and bring to a rolling boil.

Place the egg yolks in a liquidiser and blend. Then, with the motor running slowly, pour the hot vinegar and butter mixture into the liquidiser in a thin stream through the lid.

Pour the sauce into a bowl and leave for 3 minutes, stirring occasionally. If the sauce has not thickened enough, pour it back into the pan and stir constantly over the lowest possible heat until it thickens.

Add the chopped tarragon and season with the salt, pepper and lemon juice. Serve immediately.

Hot or Cold Pickled Onions

EVERY MONTH AS A CHILD, I was woken by the smell of vinegar boiling on a hot stove below my bedroom. It was pickled onion day, and my father was pickling tonnes of onions. Left in a jar for just a week, they're fab. Love them or hate them, we used to eat them all the time with pork pie – a must. I had to stop eating them, though, when I started on the girl front, but hey – you can't have everything!

SERVES 4

Cold:
215g (7½oz) table salt
2.5 litres (4½ pints) water
1kg (2lb 4oz) shallots or small
* onions*
600ml (1 pint) malt vinegar

Hot:
1kg (2lb 4oz) shallots or small
* onions*
100g (3½oz) table salt
800ml (1 pint 9fl oz) malt vinegar

For cold – or uncooked – pickled onions, mix half the salt with half the water and add the shallots or onions. Leave overnight.

Drain and peel the onions and make up the same brine with the remaining salt and water. Leave the onions in this mixture for about 3 days.

Drain the shallots again, and place them in pickling jars that have been sterilised, then pour over the vinegar. Cover, seal and label, then leave for 3 months before eating.

For hot – or cooked – pickled onions, put the onions in a saucepan of water and bring to the boil. Boil for 3-4 minutes. Drain and peel the onions and place on a tray. Dust all over with the salt and leave for a day.

Wash the onions well and simmer in a pan in the vinegar for 8 minutes before placing them in sterilised jars, covered in vinegar. Cover, seal and label, then leave for 3 weeks before eating.

Mum's Gravy

THANKS, MUM, for the best gravy recipe I know.

SERVES 4-6

100ml (3½fl oz) vegetable cooking
  water
2 white onions, sliced
25g butter
4 tsp Bisto powder
150ml (5fl oz) red wine
¼ tsp mustard powder
1 tsp cornflour
1 tsp Marmite

Remove the roasted meat from the roasting tray and pour off any excess fat. Add the vegetable water to the remaining juices in the tray and slowly simmer over a low heat on the stove top.

In a separate pan, fry the onions in the butter to give a lot of colour. Dissolve the Bisto in 600ml (1 pint) of hot water. Pour this into with the roasting tray with the red wine and add the onions.

In a small dish, stir the mustard powder and cornflour into a little water to make a a paste. Whisk or stir into the simmering gravy. Add the Marmite and stir in well. Pour into the sauce boat and serve as required.

Apple Sauce

THE AMERICANS EAT apple sauce by itself. I like it best with cold pork and stuffing. Mmmmmmm – delicious.

SERVES 4

225g (8oz) Bramley apples
1 tbsp brown sugar
a pinch of grated nutmeg
25g (1oz) butter

Peel, core and slice the apples and put in a pan with 4 tbsp water and the rest of the ingredients.

Cook over a gentle heat and simmer, stirring all the time, until the apples have reduced to a pulp.

Allow to cool before chilling in the fridge until you're ready to use the sauce.

Tartare Sauce

TARTARE SAUCE IS A CLASSIC accompaniment for any fish – grilled, baked or fried. It's much better if you make it yourself rather than buy it in a jar. In fact, you could make the mayonnaise yourself too, but perhaps that's a culinary step too far!

SERVES 4

200ml (7fl oz) mayonnaise
1 tbsp chopped capers
1 tbsp chopped gherkins
1 tbsp chopped parsley
1 tbsp chopped tarragon
1 tbsp chopped dill
juice of ½ lemon
salt and pepper, to taste

Combine all the ingredients together and blend well.

Chill in the fridge until ready to use.

PUDDINGS

Apple Pie and Custard

WHAT CAN I SAY? Just look at the picture and give it a go. I promise you won't be disappointed.

SERVES 4-6

675g (1lb 8oz) ready-made
    shortcrust pastry
700g (1lb 9oz) cooking apples
    (Bramleys)
100g (3½oz) caster sugar, plus
    extra for sprinkling
finely grated rind and juice
    of ½ lemon
25g (1oz) butter, plus extra for
    greasing
powdered cinnamon (optional)
1 egg, beaten

Custard:
1 vanilla pod
300ml (½ pint) milk
300ml (½ pint) double cream
6 egg yolks
100g (3½oz) caster sugar

Butter a 22cm (8½ inch) pie dish and pre-heat the oven to 190°C/375°F/gas mark 5.

Roll out two-thirds of the pastry on a floured work surface and line the pie dish.

Peel, quarter and core the apples, then slice them thickly into a bowl to which three-quarters of the sugar and all the lemon juice have been added. Stir gently to mix.

Put the apple slices and sugar into the pastry-lined pie dish. Dot with a little butter and a sprinkle of cinnamon powder.

Roll out the remaining pastry and put it on top of the apples. Seal and crimp the edges well and then make a small hole in the top to allow the steam to escape.

Make decorations from any pastry trimmings (I like doing a few leaves) and seal them with a little water. Brush with the beaten egg, dredge with the remaining caster sugar and then bake for 35-40 minutes, until the fruit is tender and the top is golden brown.

For the custard, split open the vanilla pod and scrape the seeds out into a heavy-based saucepan. Add the vanilla pod, milk and cream and bring slowly to the boil.

Place the egg yolks and sugar in a bowl and whisk together until they lighten in colour.

Pour the infused milk and cream on to the eggs, whisking well. Return the mixture to the pan. Place the pan over a low heat and cook the custard for about 5 minutes, stirring all the time, until it thickens slightly and coats the back of the spoon. Do not boil or the custard will curdle. Strain through a sieve and serve with the warm apple pie.

Apple Charlotte

THOUGHT TO HONOUR Queen Charlotte, the wife of George III, this can be one of two kinds of dessert: either cold ('iced') or hot. It can be made using raspberries and pears as well. I love this with custard, not 'crème anglaise', but proper British Birds custard.

SERVES 6

1kg (2lb 4oz) Bramley apples (it
  must be Bramley)
200g (7oz) butter
125g (4½oz) caster sugar
4 tbsp smooth apricot jam
10 thin slices of white bread
juice of 1 lemon

Pre-heat the oven to 180°C/350°F/gas mark 4. Peel and core the Bramley apples, then slice them.

In a large pan, melt 25g (1oz) of the butter and add the sugar and apples. Cover and, over a gentle heat, cook for about 10 minutes, stirring occasionally.

Remove the lid and cook for a further 5-10 minutes, until the apples form a smooth purée, stirring regularly. Stir in the jam and allow to cool.

Meanwhile, melt the remaining butter and cut the crusts off the bread. Cut the bread slices in half and then cut each half into 4 slices to make small fingers. Dip each finger of bread into the melted butter and use to line the mould, reserving some for the lid (you can use individual moulds or one large one).

Once the mould is lined, spoon in the apple purée and top with more bread that has been dipped in melted butter. Place in the oven for 30 minutes, or until the bread is golden brown on top.

Remove from the oven and allow to cool slightly. Carefully turn the moulds out and serve with custard.

Syrup Sponge with Custard

PURISTS WILL SAY, 'Steamed pudding in a microwave? You've got to be joking!'. But if, like me, you can't wait to taste your pud, then try this recipe. It takes a few minutes to cook, a few to prepare and a few to eat – I know, because I've made it on *Ready, Steady, Cook* and another presenter ate the whole bloody lot!

SERVES 4

150g (5½oz) plain flour
1 tsp baking powder
125g (4½oz) butter, melted
125g (4½oz) caster sugar
2 eggs
zest and juice of 2 small lemons
milk
vegetable oil, for greasing

To serve:

4 tbsp golden syrup, or jam
  if preferred
custard (see page 108)

Sieve together the flour and baking powder.

Tip the butter, sugar, eggs and flour and baking powder mix into a food processor and mix to a paste.

Add the lemon juice and zest and continue to mix, adding enough milk to make a dropping consistency.

Spoon the mixture into a greased 1.2 litre (2 pint) basin (suitable for the microwave). Cover and microwave on full power for 4 minutes, or until the sponge begins to shrink from the side and is springy to the touch.

Leave to stand for 2-3 minutes before turning out and serving with golden syrup or jam, and custard.

Warm Blackberries with Cheat's Brown Bread Ice Cream

WHEN IN SEASON, blackberries are one of my favourite foods. I like them best with nothing much done to them – as here. Brown Bread Ice Cream is traditional (well, since Victorian times), but this is the quick, 'cheat's' way to make it.

SERVES 4

500g (1lb 2oz) fresh blackberries
1½ tbsp caster sugar
sprigs of fresh mint (optional)

Ice cream:
2 slices brown bread
150ml (5fl oz) vanilla ice cream

Pre-heat the oven to 200°C/400°F/gas mark 6. Place the sliced bread in a blender and reduce to crumbs, then place on an oven tray and bake for 10 minutes. Allow to cool and rub together in your hands to break up the larger pieces.

Heat a small pan on the stove, then add the blackberries and sugar. Sauté for about 1 minute, until the berries are warm but not too mashed. Spoon the berries into the serving bowls, top with a scoop of vanilla ice cream, then sprinkle the breadcrumbs over the ice cream. Serve with a sprig of mint on top of the ice cream.

Summer Fruit Pudding

ANOTHER CLASSIC PUD, but most people are put off making it as they think it needs to be kept in the fridge for a fortnight with a brick on the top. This alternative recipe is a tribute to my mother. It can be eaten straight away.

SERVES 4-6

½ punnet each of strawberries (hulled), blackberries and redcurrants
400g (14oz) mixed frozen fruit, defrosted
approx. 125g (4½oz) caster sugar
15 slices of white bread
vegetable oil, for greasing

Quarter half of the fresh strawberries and add to three-quarters of the frozen fruit. Add 50g (1¾oz) caster sugar. Place the rest of the frozen fruit in the blender and purée. Add more sugar to taste.

Remove the crusts from the bread and line 4-6 small moulds with a little oil and then with cling film. Cut a bread circle for the base, slices for the sides and a circle for the top, dipping the bread in the fruit purée on one side before placing it in the mould. Fill the centre with the strawberry mixture, blackberries, redcurrants and purée and press well. Top with bread. Remove each pudding from the mould and place on a plate. Remove the cling film. Spoon over the sauce and garnish with the remaining strawberries.

Baked Rice Pudding

SCHOOL DINNERS always seemed to include a milk pudding such as rice pudding, tapioca or sago, all of which will probably have put you off them for life. But rice pudding's reputation has been knocked by the lack of thought and care put into making it over time.

SERVES 4

100g (3½oz) short-grain pudding rice
450ml (16fl oz) milk
450ml (16fl oz) double cream
1 vanilla pod, split (optional)
75g (2¾oz) caster sugar
a little nutmeg
25g (1oz) butter, plus extra for
  greasing

Pre-heat the oven to 180°C/350°F/gas mark 4

Lightly butter a pudding basin or oven-proof dish about 1-1.8 litres (2-3 pints) in size.

Wash the rice under cold water and allow to drain.

Bring the milk and cream to the boil with the vanilla pod (if using) and add the rice and sugar. Stir well.

Pour into the oven dish and grate a little nutmeg over the top. Dot with knobs of butter.

Bake for about 15 minutes, then lower the temperature to 150°C/300°F/gas mark 2, and bake for a further 1¼ hours. It should be golden brown on top, and creamy underneath.

Spotted Dick and Custard

FOR ME, THIS DESSERT should always be made with lemon and currants, and should not be mucked about with too much. The pudding is usually made as a roly-poly pudding, but it's difficult to find a steamer big enough. A basin is easier. The 'spotted', by the way, is a reference to the raisins dotted through the sponge.

SERVES 4

butter for greasing
350g (12oz) plain flour
2 tbsp baking powder
150g (5½oz) shredded suet
75g (2¾oz) caster sugar
125g (4½oz) currants
75ml (2½fl oz) milk
75ml (2½fl oz) single cream
25g (1oz) butter, melted
juice and zest of 2 lemons

To serve:
custard (see page 108)

Butter a 1-litre (1¾ pint) pudding basin.

Place all the dry ingredients in a bowl. Separately, mix together the milk and cream. Add the melted butter to the dry ingredients and then stir in the lemon juice and zest. While stirring, slowly add enough of the milk and cream mixture to create a dropping consistency.

Pour the mixture into the prepared pudding basin, cover and place in a colander over a pan of boiling water for about 1 hour, until cooked.

Turn the pudding out of the basin and serve it, cut into wedges, with hot custard.

Rhubarb and Ginger Crumble

WHILE FILMING, I have visited the famous 'rhubarb triangle', which runs around Leeds, Wakefield and Morley in Yorkshire. It is well worth a visit, as you can see rhubarb growing in forcing sheds. The plants grow in complete darkness for about six to eight weeks, and you can actually hear the rhubarb growing; it sounds like two wellies rubbing together. Harvesting is the best bit: it is done, by candlelight, by hand to give the stalks their unique colour and flavour. Sadly, forced rhubarb production has declined, as it is so labour-intensive and expensive. But if you see it growing and taste it, you will be a rhubard convert for life.

SERVES 6

Filling:

10 sticks of young rhubarb
4 tbsp water
115g (4oz) caster sugar
3 tbsp stem ginger in syrup,
    chopped

Crumble:

100g (3½oz) butter, softened
100g (3½oz) demerara sugar
175-200g (6-7oz) plain flour

Pre-heat the oven to 180°C/350°F/gas mark 4.

Cut the rhubarb into 5cm (2 inch) slices and place on a baking tray. Sprinkle with the water and caster sugar and roast for 10 minutes.

Once the rhubarb is cooked, remove it from the oven and sprinkle the ginger over it. Mix together and place in an ovenproof dish about 3-4cm (1¼-1½ inches) deep.

In a separate bowl, mix the butter and demerara sugar together until the mixture resembles breadcrumbs. Then mix in the flour to make the crumble.

Sprinkle the crumble over the rhubarb and bake for 10 minutes. Remove and allow to cool slightly before serving with ice cream or double cream.

Banana Custard Soufflé

BANANAS AND CUSTARD was the best dessert ever when you were growing up, but when you reach a certain age you never seem to eat it again, apart from when you're ill. I've played around here with a real British classic – this is a great dish to serve as a bit of fun at a dinner party, or just for a cosy dinner for two.

SERVES 2

50g (1¾oz) butter
3 tbsp caster sugar
4 egg whites
finely grated zest of 2 oranges
8 tbsp fresh custard (bought-in or homemade – see page 108)
3 medium bananas

To serve:
100ml (3½fl oz) vanilla ice cream (optional)

Pre-heat the oven to 180°C/350°F/gas mark 4.

Rub 2 ramekin dishes with half the butter and sprinkle with 1 tablespoon of the caster sugar. Whisk the egg whites and, when they are stiff, beat in a tablespoon of the caster sugar.

Mix the orange zest into the custard and then gently fold in the whisked egg whites. Spoon the mixture into the prepared ramekins and place on an oven tray. Bake for 15-20 minutes.

While the soufflés are cooking, peel the bananas and cut in half lengthways.

Heat up a non-stick pan and add the remaining butter. When it's nut-brown, add the remaining sugar and the halved bananas. Fry them on both sides, taking care not to break them and to give them a nice golden colour.

To serve, place the warm bananas on the plate, serve the soufflé on the side and, if you dare, a dollop of vanilla ice cream on the side, too!

Baked Cheesecake

AMERICANS HAVE MASTERED the art of making cheesecakes, but they started here and were taken across the Atlantic. This is a great recipe, light in texture and delicious served with caramelised bananas.

SERVES 6

a little butter for greasing
1 x 25cm (10 inch) bought sponge
  flan case
200g (7oz) caster sugar
finely grated zest of 3 lemons
4 tbsp cornflour
3 tbsp sultanas, soaked in a
  little bourbon
850g (1lb 14oz) full-fat soft
  cream cheese
3 medium eggs
1 vanilla pod
50ml (2fl oz) Jack Daniel's or
  bourbon, to taste (optional)
375ml (13fl oz) double cream

To serve:
10 small bananas
25g (1oz) butter
2 tbsp sugar
caramel sauce or maple syrup

Pre-heat the oven to 180°C/350°F/gas mark 4.

Butter a 25cm (10 inch) loose-bottomed cake tin. Cut the sponge horizontally into 2 discs. Use one to line the buttered cake tin (I'd suggest using the other to line a trifle).

In a bowl, mix together the sugar, lemon zest, cornflour and sultanas using a wooden spoon, then beat in the cream cheese. Add the eggs, one by one, beating constantly until all of them are well incorporated.

Slice open the vanilla pod, remove the seeds with a sharp knife, and place them in the cream cheese mixture. Add the Jack Daniel's, if using, and mix everything together well. Add the cream and beat well until the mixture is smooth. Pour gently over the sponge base in the cake tin.

Sit the tin in a baking tray filled with 2-3mm (⅛ inch) of warm water to help create steam during cooking. Bake for 50 minutes, until the top is golden. Remove from the oven and leave to cool and set completely before removing from the tin.

Just before serving, peel the bananas and fry in the butter and sugar until brown and slightly caramelised.

Serve the cheesecake cut into wedges, with the bananas and a drizzle of caramel sauce or maple syrup.

Sherry Trifle with Raspberries

TRIFLES ARE ANCIENT – they go back to medieval times. Some contained jelly and some used syllabub as a topping instead of cream. You can also use sponge fingers or macaroons instead of the sponge.

SERVES 6

70g (2½oz) raspberry jam
225g (8oz) plain sponge cake, sliced
150ml (5fl oz) sherry
200g (7oz) fresh raspberries
custard (made with 600ml/1 pint milk – double the quantity on page 108)
zest of 2 oranges
400ml (14fl oz) double cream
25g (1oz) toasted flaked almonds

Spread the jam over the slices of sponge cake and place in the bottom of a large glass dish, or divide evenly among six tall glasses.

Pour the sherry over the cake and sprinkle the fresh raspberries evenly over the top.

When you have made the custard, pass it through a sieve, add the orange zest and allow to cool. Pour over the sponge and fruit.

Whip the double cream and either pipe it over the top of the trifle or, if you are like my mother, who does have a piping bag (although it's collecting dust at the back of a drawer in the kitchen), spread it on and spike it with a fork.

Cover and refrigerate overnight, and sprinkle with the toasted flaked almonds just before serving.

Yorkshire Curd Tart

MY AUNTY'S FAVOURITE, and thought to originate from the 13th century, this is otherwise known as cheesecake.

SERVES 8-12

300g (10½oz) pack of sweet
  shortcrust pastry
butter, for greasing
rice or baking beans

Filling:
500ml (18fl oz) whipping cream
8 egg yolks
75g (2¾oz) caster sugar
1 tsp ground allspice

Pre-heat the oven to 180°C/350°F/gas mark 4. Roll out the pastry and line a greased flan dish, leaving any excess pastry hanging over the edge until it is cooked. Line with greaseproof paper and fill with rice or baking beans, then leave to rest in the fridge for 20-30 minutes.

Bake for 15 minutes. Once the pastry shell is cooked, remove from the oven and take the greaseproof paper and rice or baking beans out. Turn the oven down to 130°C/250°F/gas mark 1.

To make the filling, bring the cream to the boil and, in a bowl, mix the egg yolks with the caster sugar and half the allspice. Pour the cream on to the egg mixture, being careful not to let the yolks curdle, then pass through a sieve. Pour into the cooked pastry case. Sprinkle with the remaining allspice and bake in the oven for 23-45 minutes, until the custard is set. Remove from the oven and allow to cool. Cut into slices and serve at room temperature.

Lemon Syllabub

NOT A REAL SYLLABUB made with egg yolks and sugar, this was invented when I was filming *Housecall* for the Beeb. I think it is a fantastic recipe, quick to make and really tasty to eat.

SERVES 4-6

100g (3½oz) caster sugar
juice and zest of 2 lemons
2-3 tbsp brandy
600ml (1 pint) double cream

Whisk together the caster sugar, lemon juice, zest and brandy.

In another bowl, whisk the cream until thick, then slowly whisk in the lemon mixture. Pour into wine glasses and refrigerate overnight.

Serve with ratafia biscuits or brandy snaps.

Black Forest Gâteau

THIS IS OBVIOUSLY GERMAN, but it has always been very popular here. My version is the same as the classic, but with the addition of chocolate shards around the edge. I love it, but I only use tinned cherries. Who wouldn't love it? Chocolate sponge, double cream and cherries all piled up, with even more chocolate…

SERVES 4

For the sponge:

6 eggs

150g (5½oz) caster sugar

125g (4½oz) self-raising flour

25g (1oz) cocoa powder

Filling and topping:

3 x 425g cans black cherries

2 tbsp cornflour

a good dash of Kirsch

750ml (1 pint 9fl oz) double cream, whipped

50g (1¾oz) toasted flaked almonds

Chocolate shards:

300g (10½oz) dark chocolate, broken into pieces

Pre-heat the oven to 180°C/350°F/gas mark 4. Grease and line a deep 30cm (12 inch) round cake tin.

For the sponge, break the eggs into a mixing bowl, add the sugar and whisk well until it reaches the ribbon stage, or is very light and fluffy. Carefully fold in the sifted flour and cocoa powder. Pour the mix into the prepared tin and bake for about 40-45 minutes, until cooked.

Turn out on to a wire rack and leave to cool.

For the filling, drain the cherries, reserving the juice. Put the juice into a pan and bring to the boil. Meanwhile, mix the cornflour with a little water to make a paste. When the cherry juice is boiling, mix the cornflour paste into it. Strain through a sieve over the cherries, also pouring through the Kirsch. Leave to one side to cool.

Cut the sponge into three layers using a sharp knife. Sandwich the three layers together using the whipped cream, half the cherries and all the almonds.

Melt the chocolate, spread on to a tray lined with cling film, and place in the fridge to set. When the chocolate is set, break it into large shards and stick them randomly around the edge of the cake.

Pile the remaining cherries on top of the cake and serve.

Chocolate Mousse

ANGEL DELIGHT, BLANCMANGE, strawberry and orange jelly and chocolate mousse – all great foods we used to eat as kids. I remember the blancmange my gran used to make. It was bright pink and was made in those old jelly moulds. I'm not giving you the recipe for that, as the best is out of a packet. Another great treat, of course, was chocolate mousse. This, I suppose, is the grown-up version.

SERVES 6

200g (7oz) dark chocolate (70% cocoa solids), broken into pieces
125ml (4fl oz) warm water
3 large eggs, separated
40g (1½oz) golden caster sugar

To serve:
a little whipped cream

Place the broken-up chocolate and warm water in a large, heat-proof bowl and sit it over a pan of barely simmering water, making sure the bowl doesn't touch the water.

Keep the heat at its lowest setting and allow the chocolate to melt slowly – it should take about 6 minutes.

Remove it from the heat and stir thoroughly until the chocolate is smooth and glossy. Let the mixture cool before adding the egg yolks. Mix them in thoroughly with a wooden spoon.

In a clean bowl, whisk the egg whites to the soft-peak stage. Whisk in the sugar gradually, then continue whisking until the whites are glossy. Using a metal spoon, fold the egg whites into the chocolate mixture. Take care not to knock the air out of the egg whites.

Divide the mousse among six ramekins or glasses and chill for at least 2 hours. Serve with a dollop of whipped cream on top.

Peach Melba

THE ORIGINAL PECHE MELBA was created by the great Savoy chef, Escoffier, for Dame Nellie Melba. I have made a few changes.

SERVES 2

1 small tin peach halves
2 tbsp apricot coulis
2 brandy snap baskets
2 scoops vanilla ice cream
4 tbsp raspberry coulis
25g (1oz) fresh raspberries
a sprig of mint
2 chocolate cigarette curls

Drain the peaches. Pour 1 tbsp apricot coulis on to the centre of each of 2 plates and add a brandy snap basket to each, pressing it down to secure it in place. Top with a scoop of ice cream and a peach half.

Pour 2 tbsp raspberry coulis around each peach half. Garnish with fresh raspberries, mint and a chocolate curl.

Peaches and Ice Cream

TINNED PEACHES AND BOUGHT-IN ICE CREAM – how fab. But here's a vanilla ice cream recipe if you want to have a go at making it yourself. This is a sort of Peach Melba without the Melba – and very, very me.

SERVES 4

1 large tin of peaches in syrup

Vanilla ice cream:
500ml (18fl oz) milk
500ml (18fl oz) double cream
2 vanilla pods, split
225g (8oz) caster sugar
10 egg yolks

To make the ice cream, place the milk and cream in a saucepan and add the seeds from the vanilla pods. Slowly bring to a simmer. Meanwhile, whisk the sugar and egg yolks together in a large bowl.

Pour the hot milk and cream mixture on to the eggs, whisking all the time. Return the pan to a very low heat and keep stirring until the mixture coats the back of a wooden spoon. (A quick chef's tip: keep stirring until most of the bubbles disappear; do not boil. The bubbles disappearing is a sign the mixture is starting to thicken.)

Freeze in an ice cream machine or a metal container. If you use the latter, freeze for about 1 hour, then take out of the freezer and beat with a whisk to break up the ice crystals and re-freeze for at least 3 hours.

Serve the drained peaches with a scoop of ice cream.

Arctic Roll

I SPOKE TO A LOAD OF CHEFS one day, while cooking, about food for this book. When asked what dessert they used to eat as kids, this was the one that brought back the best memories. The hardest thing was trying to replicate that frozen pud your mother used to buy from the shops, and the best way that I have found of doing this is to use a piece of drainpipe. Yes, a piece of drainpipe! I'll say no more; just read on and have a go.

SERVES 4

1 x 500ml tub vanilla ice cream
2 punnets of fresh raspberries
3-4 tbsp raspberry jam
2 tbsp chopped mint
icing sugar

Sponge:
butter, for greasing
3 eggs
75g (2¾oz) caster sugar, plus extra
  for sprinkling
75g (2¾oz) plain flour, plus extra
  for dusting

Pre-heat the oven to 190°C/375°F/gas mark 5. Start the sponge by lining a 30cm by 20cm (12 by 8 inch) shallow Swiss roll tin with butter and greaseproof paper. Whisk together the eggs and caster sugar until they reach ribbon stage, then sift in the flour and gently fold it in. Once the mixture is well blended, pour it into the tin and push it to the edges, levelling with a palette knife. Bake in the pre-heated oven for 8-10 minutes, until golden brown. Once cooked, you should be able to test it with your finger by pressing lightly on the top; if it springs back, then it's cooked.

Remove from the oven and tip out on to a clean tea towel sprinkled with caster sugar. Remove the greaseproof paper from underneath the sponge, cover with a dampened tea towel and allow to cool.

For the ice cream, you need a piece of clean drainpipe, 30cm (12 inches) long and 12-15cm (4½-6 inches) in diameter. Place the ice cream in a bowl and fork in the raspberries, leaving half a punnet for garnish. Fill the drainpipe with ice cream. Press down well, then put in the freezer.

Spread the sponge evenly all over with jam, then sprinkle over the mint. Use a hot cloth to remove the ice cream from the drainpipe, by wrapping the cloth around the outside and then pushing the ice cream out from one end. Place the ice cream on the sponge and roll the sponge around it by pulling the tea towel towards you.

Once the sponge covers all the ice cream, trim off any excess sponge and put the roll on a plate with a dusting of icing sugar, the remaining raspberries and a sprig of mint.

To serve, cut into slices. I bet you never thought you'd be able to make this one at home!

CAKES

Scones

SCONES (LIKE 'STONES') or scones (like 'swans')? Say it how you want, but the best way of eating them is, of course, with clotted cream and jam. Scottish by origin, they can be made with mashed potato, and they can be griddled or baked in the oven – there are so many variations.

SERVES 4

225g (8oz) self-raising flour,
  plus extra for dusting
30g (1oz) caster sugar
a pinch of salt
30g (1oz) butter, diced, plus extra
  for greasing
150ml (5fl oz) milk

Glaze:
1 egg, lightly beaten
a little milk

To serve:
clotted cream
strawberry jam

Pre-heat the oven to 220°C/425°F/gas mark 7.

Put the flour, caster sugar and salt in a food processor and blitz briefly to mix. Add the butter and blend again until the mixture forms crumbs. Add the milk in a thin stream while mixing. stopping when the dough forms a ball. It should be moist, but not sticking to the sides.

Turn the mixture out on to a heavily floured surface, and form into a ball, then press gently into a 2cm- (¾ inch) thick round. Cut out the scones using a 5cm round cutter and put on to a greased baking tray. Brush the scones with the beaten egg.

Bake for 12-14 minutes. Remove and allow to cool slightly on a rack. Serve, while still warm, with clotted cream and strawberry jam.

Shortbread

WHO WOULD HAVE THOUGHT IT? The origins of shortbread appear to be 500 to 600 years old. It was made as a festive treat, and was not meant to be dunked into your coffee, but how times have changed! The best shortbread is to be found, I think, in Perthshire in Scotland. Recently, the Scottish Association of Master Bakers challenged the Government, which wanted to change shortbread from being a special confection into a common biscuit! What is the world coming to?

MAKES 20 BISCUITS

225g (8oz) chilled unsalted butter, plus extra for greasing
225g plain flour
60g (2¼oz) caster sugar, plus extra for dusting
a pinch of salt
1 tsp vanilla extract

Pre-heat the oven to 180°C/350°F/gas mark 4. Butter a baking sheet.

Dice the butter and put it into a mixing bowl to soften. Sift the flour on top with the caster sugar, salt and vanilla extract. Rub together gently to form into a ball (alternatively, blitz all the ingredients in a food processor until they form a ball).

Lightly flour the work surface and then roll out the shortbread mixture until it is about 5mm (¼ inch) thick. Using a fork, prick all over the surface.

With a sharp knife, cut the shortbread into fingers about 5cm (2 inches) long and 1.5cm (½ inch) wide. Carefully lift on to the buttered baking sheet and rest in the fridge for 30 minutes or so. Dust with a little caster sugar before baking.

Bake the shortbread for 20 minutes, or until golden brown and firm to the touch. Leave until completely cooled before removing from the baking sheet.

Chocolate Biscuit Cake

ANY KID'S FAVOURITE, big or little. Use this recipe as a starting point and experiment with other combinations of biscuits, dried fruits and nuts. Ginger biscuits or amaretti work well for a more grown-up version.

SERVES 8

125g (4½oz) dark chocolate, broken into pieces
1 tbsp golden syrup
125g (4½oz) butter
125g (4½oz) digestive biscuits, roughly crushed
100g (3½oz) ready-to-eat, dried apricots, chopped
100g (3½oz) raisins
100g (3½oz) glacé cherries, halved
60g (2¼oz) shelled hazelnuts, roughly chopped

Line a 450g (1lb) loaf tin with cling film, leaving enough to fold over the top when the tin is full.

Melt the chocolate, syrup and butter in a bowl in the microwave, giving it a stir to make sure all the ingredients are well blended.

Add the crushed biscuits, dried fruits and hazelnuts and stir well.

Tip the mixture into the loaf tin and shake to level it off. Fold over the cling film and put it in the fridge to set – this will take 1-2 hours.

This mixture will keep for up to 2 weeks in the fridge, if you can resist temptation for that long.

To serve, turn it out onto a plate, carefully peel off the cling film and slice. The cake is very rich, so try thin slices at first.

Granny's Victoria Sponge

MY GRAN USED TO swear by this one and my auntie by the other one (see page 136), so you choose – they're both great.

MAKES A 20CM SPONGE

200g (7oz) unsalted butter,
  softened, plus extra for greasing
200g (7oz) caster sugar
1 tsp vanilla extract
4 eggs
200g (7oz) self-raising flour, sifted
  plus extra for dusting

To serve:

double cream, whipped
raspberry jam
icing sugar

Pre-heat the oven to 190°C/375°F/gas mark 5.

Lightly grease and flour 2 x 20cm (8 inch) ponge tins, at least 4cm (1½ inches) deep. Line the bases with parchment paper.

Beat the butter and caster sugar together until well creamed. Add the vanilla extract. Gently mix the eggs together in a small bowl, then add, little by little, to the butter mixture. Once all the eggs have been combined, fold in the sifted flour and divide the mixture between the tins.

Bake for 20-25 minutes, until well risen and golden brown on top. Once cooked, turn out and leave to cool on a wire rack.

Fill with whipped double cream and raspberry jam, and sprinkle with a dusting of icing sugar.

Auntie's Sponge

GRANNY'S SPONGE IS the classic creamed sponge, while Aunty's is a whisked sponge. This one won't last as long as the other, but it's just as delicious.

MAKES A 20CM SPONGE

6 medium eggs
175g (6oz) caster sugar
175g (6oz) plain flour, sifted
50g (1¾oz) butter, melted, plus
  extra for greasing

To serve:
double cream, whipped
raspberry jam
icing sugar

Pre-heat the oven to 200°C (400°F) Gas Mark 6.

Grease and flour a deep 20cm (8 inch) sponge tin.

Place the eggs and sugar in a bowl and whisk to the ribbon stage. This will take a few minutes, so be patient.

Once the mixture has doubled in volume, fold in the flour. Carefully, but quickly, fold in the butter at the same time.

Pour into the tin and bake for 30 minutes. Test with a skewer in the centre – if it comes out clean, the sponge is ready.

Allow to cool for 10 minutes before turning out.

Finish by cutting in half horizontally and filling with whipped cream and jam. Sprinkle with a dusting of icing sugar if you want to – I would!

Banana Cake

THE GREAT THING I find about this recipe is that the bananas help keep the cake nice and moist. A lot of banana cake recipes contain nuts such as almonds or walnuts, but I think it's nicer plain.

MAKES 1 CAKE

4 large ripe bananas
125g (4½oz) butter, softened, plus
 extra for greasing
250g (9oz) self-raising flour
200g (7oz) caster sugar
3 medium eggs
3 tbsp golden syrup

Pre-heat the oven to 170°C/340°F/gas mark 4.

Butter a large loaf tin.

Peel the bananas and put them into a food processor. Blend for 10 seconds to break them up.

Add all the other ingredients and blend again for 10 seconds. Scrape down the sides and blend again for a few seconds to mix everything in.

Spoon the mixture into the buttered loaf tin and spread evenly. Bake for 1¼-1½ hours, until well risen and firm to the touch. At this point, insert a small knife to test the cake; if it is pulled out clean and the tip is not wet, then the cake is ready.

Remove from the oven and leave to rest for 10 minutes before turning out of the tin and placing on a wire rack to cool. Serve the cake warm.

Chocolate Roulade

A CLASSIC, sometimes served as a yule log at Christmas time, but I like it all year round. Fill it with whipped cream and chocolate as here, with cream on its own, or with cream and fresh berries such as raspberries or blackberries.

SERVES 4-6

sunflower oil for greasing
175g (6oz) plain chocolate, broken
into pieces
6 eggs, separated
175g (6oz) caster sugar
icing sugar for dusting

Filling:
90g (3¼oz) plain chocolate, broken
into pieces
300ml (½ pint) double cream,
whipped until thick

Pre-heat the oven to 180°C/350°F/gas mark 4.

Lightly grease a 30cm x 20cm (12 x 8 inch) shallow Swiss roll tin with sunflower oil and line with baking parchment.

Put the chocolate into a small, heat-proof bowl over a pan of hot water and heat gently, stirring occasionally, to melt the chocolate. Leave to cool.

Combine the egg yolks and sugar in a large bowl and whisk together until light and creamy. Add the cooled chocolate and stir to blend evenly.

In a separate bowl, whisk the egg whites until stiff but not dry. Carefully fold into the chocolate mixture.

Turn the chocolate mixture into the tin, tilting it so that the mixture spreads evenly into the corners. Bake for 20 minutes, or until firm to the touch.

Remove from the oven. Place a clean, dry tea towel on the cake, and on top of this lay another tea towel that has been soaked in cold water and well wrung out. Leave in a cool place for 8 hours.

For the filling, put the chocolate into a heat-proof bowl over a pan of hot water and heat gently, stirring occasionally, to melt the chocolate. Cool.

Remove the tea towels from the sponge and turn it out on to a piece of baking parchment that has been liberally sprinkled with sifted icing sugar. Peel the lining paper from the cake.

Spread the melted chocolate over the cake, then spread the whipped cream evenly on top. Roll up the cake from a long edge, using the sugared paper to help lift and roll it forward. Dust the roulade with more sifted icing sugar before serving.

Chocolate Cornflake Cakes

I DON'T CARE WHAT all my cheffy mates think of me for putting this in a British book. Frosties, Cornflakes or Rice Krispies, whichever you choose, I bet these little cakes won't even be able to set in the fridge before they're eaten. I love them made either with a chocolate bar or a Mars Bar.

MAKES 12

50g (1¾oz) butter
100g dark chocolate, broken
  into pieces
5 tbsp golden syrup
80g (2¾oz) cornflakes

Place the butter and the chocolate pieces in a pan with the golden syrup and slowly melt over a low heat. When the mixture has melted and amalgamated, stir in the cornflakes.

Place paper cases on a tray and fill each one with a tablespoon of the mixture. Put in the fridge to set.

Carrot and Cinnamon Cake

CARROTS WERE USED as a cheap substitute for expensive imported dried fruit for hundreds of years. Mrs Beeton's recipes are fantastic, but it's the Americans who I think serve this best, with a dollop of crème fraîche or soured cream.

SERVES 8

300ml (½ pint) sunflower oil, plus extra for greasing
225g (8oz) soft brown sugar
4 medium eggs
175g (6oz) golden syrup
350g (12oz) self-raising flour
2 tbsp cinnamon powder
1 tsp bicarbonate of soda
275g (9½oz) grated carrot

Pre-heat the oven to 180°C/350°F/gas mark 4.

Grease 2 x 500g (1lb) loaf tins with sunflower oil.

Put the oil, sugar, eggs and golden syrup into a food processor and then add the flour, cinnamon, bicarbonate of soda and grated carrots.

Blend everything together, pour into the loaf tins and bake in the pre-heated oven for 40-50 minutes. Once cooked, leave to rest for 10-15 minutes before turning out of the tins.

Whoever is quickest gets a slice. Dive in!

Index

oven
centre.

3.

decorate onto with any spare pastry.
ontop, make two slits onto and bake in
hot oven for 25 minutes, and then in a
hot oven for 15 minutes.
    °C (Gas →)
    °C (Gas 5)

Roll each piece
Put one on a
ixture in the
Put the top on
round the edge. Trim edges

ham is meat too.
chicken in the pie so
brown and it has a good
ed pastry ontop. ?

            M.

You can do better than this James.

Texture.
Nutritive Value